"At a time when Black students continue to deal with implicit and explicit racism inside and outside of schools, this is a much-needed resource that helps them to understand, heal, and act in the face of racial stress and trauma. This invaluable workbook has powerful tools, resources, and strategies for anyone working with Black students who want to see them thrive and experience joy."

—**Tyrone C. Howard**, Pritzker Family Endowed Professor in the School of Education and Information Studies at UCLA

"This practical, uplifting guide provides evidence-based tools and realistic examples to help Black teens understand and cope with racial stress."

—**Marianne Celano, PhD, ABPP**, professor of psychiatry at Emory University School of Medicine, and coauthor of *Something Happened in Our Town: A Child's Story about Racial Injustice*

"Post 2020, the impact of racialized trauma has been made more visible. This is a valuable workbook for all clinicians working with Black adolescents and emerging adults struggling to navigate the psychological impact of racism on themselves and their communities."

—**Frances Y. Adomako, PhD**, vice president of the WELLS Healing Center, senior clinician at Radical Healing Collaborative, and APA Minority Fellow

"I recommend this workbook for teens, teachers, parents, and anyone working with youth from minoritized backgrounds. Rooted in current psychological research, *Healing Racial Stress Workbook for Black Teens* is a powerful tool for supporting youth in the identification and deployment of cultural, social, and cognitive assets to cope with racism. The authors include relatable examples, accessible language, and concrete strategies to steer youth of color to healthy coping and resilience."

—**Stephanie J. Rowley, PhD**, developmental psychologist, and dean of the School of Education and Human Development at the University of Virginia

"Grounded in research and theory, *Healing Racial Stress Workbook for Black Teens* gives adolescents the tools and skills needed to navigate challenging racialized times. The authors reflect the critical need for Black teens to not only understand racism, but also identify its impact while employing strategies of resistance. Activities are intentionally designed for teens to discern race-related stressors, as they build on their strengths and become empowered young people."

> —**Brett Johnson Solomon, PhD**, associate professor, and chair of the child studies department at Santa Clara University

"A refreshingly engaging and evidence-informed resource for young people who have felt confused, angry, or powerless in the face of racial trauma. This workbook equips Black teens to navigate the nuances of managing the stress of racism while drawing closer to cultural pride and wholeness. I'm confident any teen that completes the activities in this workbook will discover the joy of healing and be inspired to make the world better!"

> —**Isaiah B. Pickens, PhD**, CEO of iOpening Enterprises, and former assistant director of the National Center for Child Traumatic Stress (NCTSS)

"This workbook is an excellent guide for Black youth to learn ways to manage and move through racial stress and trauma. The authors include the perfect combination of information, reflection, and activities to equip Black adolescents with a repertoire of strategies for navigating the complexities of racism in ways that honor themselves in the process. This is an essential resource for Black youth and all who care for them."

> —**Sharon Lambert, PhD**, professor of clinical-community psychology at The George Washington University

"As the aunt of Black teenagers and an educator who has dedicated her career to improving academic outcomes for Black children, I am keenly aware of the stressors adolescents face—bravely, headfirst, and often with little support. *Healing Racial Stress Workbook for Black Teens* finally provides this support. The resources and activities in this workbook create opportunities for Black adolescents to celebrate their identity, identify help in their communities, and examine the experiences and feelings they have yet to be able to name, though they feel their impact. This is a powerful workbook every Black adolescent should have access to."

> —**Miah Daughtery, EdD**, vice president of Content Advocacy-Literacy at NWEA, Chair of 826DC Board of Directors, and past middle school and high school English teacher

HEALING RACIAL STRESS WORKBOOK FOR BLACK TEENS

Skills to Help You Manage Emotions, Resist Racism & Feel Empowered

JESSICA S. HENRY, PHD

FARZANA T. SALEEM, PHD

DANA L. CUNNINGHAM, PHD

NICOLE L. CAMMACK, PHD

DANIELLE R. BUSBY, PHD

Instant Help Books

An Imprint of New Harbinger Publications, Inc.

Publisher's Note

INSTANT HELP, the Clock Logo, and NEW HARBINGER are trademarks of New Harbinger Publications, Inc.

New Harbinger Publications is an employee-owned company.

Cover design by Amy Shoup

Acquired by Elizabeth Hollis Hansen

Edited by Joyce Wu

Library of Congress Cataloging-in-Publication Data on file

Printed in the United States of America

25   24   23

10   9   8   7   6   5   4   3   2   1   First Printing

This book is dedicated to all the Black youth who are healing from racial stress and trauma, and to all the individuals who are dedicated to their healing.

Contents

contents

foreword

For many decades I have studied how parents talk to their children about race and while I see it as historically one of the most powerful ways we can protect children from racial trauma, it is not the most efficient. This field is called racial socialization and we need to make it better for families and children.

For the future journey, as parents, we must be more vulnerable in our racial storytelling, more open to answering hard questions about our racial struggles, and less worried about what others think of our racial anger. As children, we must ask more questions that disturb the racial quiet and be more relentless in our pursuit of voice. As families, we must be more explicit, rehearsed, spontaneous, practiced, and loving in preparing each other both for racial hostilities and for thriving. To be fully human, we need all the above.

The Healing Racial Stress Workbook is fundamentally what the doctor ordered to begin this journey. What Jessica Henry, Farzana Saleem, Dana Cunningham, Nicole Cammack, and Danielle Busby have accomplished is to make explicit what it takes to emotionally manage and face the truth that one's Blackness and Brownness must be embraced.

Despite our numerous theories of racial identification, identity, and socialization, we have spent far less time drawing a blueprint for how to build these foundational elements of mental well-being. This workbook makes it clear that they are all linked together. But how? It is no secret that the intention behind parents explaining how racism works to their children is so that they will be able to defend and uplift themselves despite those barriers. In effect, the parental intention is for them to learn to cope well, which they hope will lead to living, learning, and healing well.

The Healing Racial Stress Workbook moves this intention from hope towards a set of actions. It begins with not just understanding racism but also helping teenagers learn what impact racism has on their emotions, behavior, and identity. The approach of using activities and worksheets to stimulate cognitive appraisal, restructuring, and positive thinking is far more explicit than "The Talk" most families can provide.

This workbook appreciates the range of challenging perceptions, worries, and fears that adolescents navigate, but brings greater tools and awareness to the racially stressful aspects of development that school counselors and psychotherapists are too often unprepared to deliver.

If you are a caregiver, you will find this workbook enlightening because it opens up the areas that many of us were either afraid or unprepared to talk about. If you are a teenager, you will find options for problem-solving racial stress in relationships, in school, in life, and in your head. Given the rise and tensions of racial politics in the US, these options can keep you from wandering into uncomfortable racial encounters and from feeling helpless. If you are a counselor, you will find an opportunity to easily integrate these pragmatic strategies into a healthy social and emotional learning program.

I believe that one of the powerful benefits of racial socialization is to help youth emotionally regulate and buffer the stress of racial hostility. *The Healing Racial Stress Workbook* begins the work of helping teenagers build emotional regulation skills for future racial challenges, regardless of where they might show up. The journey for managing and overcoming racism is lifelong, but the skills learned from this workbook can help youth prevent racially stressful encounters from becoming traumatic ones.

—Howard C. Stevenson, Ph.D.
University of Pennsylvania

Who am I? What does it mean to be a young Black person in the United States of America today? How should I feel as I watch other Black people being killed or mistreated due to the color of their skin?

Many teens like you are exploring these exact same questions and seeking answers to them, even though they may not always talk about it. Adolescence is when you begin to explore and understand who you are, what your identity is, what your racial identity is, and what all this means to you—outside the other meanings, identities, and labels adults have placed on you.

Your racial identity may be a source of great pride for you, and it has a big impact on how you define yourself and see yourself in the world. So what happens when you experience a negative situation due to your race? Does it affect how you feel about who you are? Does it change how you see yourself? What do you do with all the thoughts, feelings, and questions that come up as a result of that negative experience?

This book explores racial stress and trauma, particularly as it relates to you as a Black adolescent and your experiences. You may have encountered racism, discrimination, and different treatment based on the color of your skin or the texture of your hair. Racial stress refers to the emotional and physical responses that you may have from a negative racial experience. A racially stressful experience becomes racial trauma if the events cause you emotional and psychological harm that threatens your integrity and safety. Racial trauma is when dangerous or frightening race-based events, stressors, or discrimination happen that "overwhelm one's coping capacity and impact quality of life and/or cause fear, helplessness, and horror" (Carter 2007). Research shows that youth experience racism, prejudice, and bias as early as three or four years old (Katz and Kofkin 1997). Trauma exposure is higher among children and adolescents of color (Roberts et al. 2011). This may be due to often-overlooked experiences of covert racism, like microaggressions and humiliation, and witnessing things happen to friends and family. Experiences like these may lead to physical and emotional distress, poor academic performance, difficulty focusing and paying attention in class, as well as symptoms in your body, like your heart racing fast or palms sweating. If you are struggling with experiences of racial stress, you may also:

- Feel isolated or alone

- Feel ignored by society and those close to you

- Think no one would understand or do anything to help you with your experiences

- Feel embarrassed

- Experience fear of retaliation

- Feel angry

We want this book to help you understand any experiences of racial stress and trauma that you may have experienced. You don't need to feel alone. When you gently explore your experiences, thoughts, and feelings, you can learn valuable tools to manage your racial stress. As you continue to make your way through this book, it will lead you through a self-guided journey of:

- Defining different types of racial stressors

- Understanding and labeling your specific experiences

- Identifying how racial stress and trauma may impact you

- Reflecting on your personal experiences to gain insight

- Learning specific strategies to help you cope with racial stress and trauma

It helps to have a quiet place to work through each of the chapters so you can think about and reflect on your personal experiences. You may notice that a lot of thoughts and emotions come up for you during this journey, and that is normal.

It is courageous to notice and sit with thoughts and emotions. It is important that you identify trusting adults you can talk to if it's too hard to handle your feelings alone. Who are the trusted adults and friends in your life that you can approach to discuss your experiences with racial stress? You may find that you have more than one person that you trust for each category, or you may find that there are some adults you always feel safe to talk to, so their name may be appropriate for more than one category. This is okay! Add as many people as you feel safe with below:

_____ is someone I can trust to share my feelings with.

_____ is someone I can trust to help me talk about my feelings.

_____ is someone who will support me if I feel overwhelmed.

Sometimes the process of sitting with thoughts and emotions allows you to have a better understanding of your experiences and helps you identify what specific coping strategies and tools you need to help you get through difficult thoughts and feelings. For many teens, this process may be uncomfortable, as you may get overwhelmed by the feeling of the emotion or stressor that you are experiencing. Having the right strategies or tools to help you manage how you're feeling is key to getting through many of life's difficulties. Can you identify a difficult time in the past? Thinking back, what helped you to get through that moment? Are there things you wished you had to get through the difficulty? Common coping strategies include tools, activities, and support from other people, and can also include words, affirmations, or positive images to help you to keep going. While coping strategies do not always fix the problem or erase it from ever happening, they do help you to manage your emotions in the moment and may even lead you closer to identifying a solution to the difficulty.

What are three words, affirmations, or images that helped you to keep going through a difficult time in the past?

1. _____

2. _____

3. _____

One way to have healthy thoughts is to practice using affirmations, which is really just a fancy way of saying positive thoughts. For example, how might you feel if every morning you looked in the mirror and said:

- "I can do hard things."

- "I am loved."

- "I am proud to be Black."

- "I am hopeful of my future."

- "My identity is valid."

- "I have family and friends who understand me and support me through this journey."

- "I am open to learning new skills for coping with racial stress."

For some teens, creating a routine of stating affirmations to themselves can lead to feeling more confident, brave, and proud. If you have never practiced this strategy, in the beginning it may feel a bit awkward to look in a mirror and state an affirmation to yourself. What you will notice is that over time it becomes easier to state the affirmation, and your thoughts about yourself and your identity may start to improve. If you are interested in trying this strategy out, here are a few steps to get you started.

Identify at least three affirmations that you would like to practice saying to yourself. You can use affirmations from the previous list or identify new affirmations. Write down the affirmations:

1. _____

2. _____

3. _____

Identify a specific day and time that you will state the words or affirmations to yourself in the mirror. Write down the day(s) and time(s):

_____

_____

How did you feel after stating these affirmations to yourself? Write down how you feel:

_____

_____

_____

We also want you to use your creativity to identify any words, affirmations, or images that motivate you. On the following page, you can draw or add a picture (from a magazine or photograph). Then you can write statements of affirmation, or even just include words that inspire you. Remember this is your space, so add colors, pictures, or whatever brings your words and images to life! We hope that when any difficult feelings come up, you can always come back to this page as a reminder of who you are and why you are working through this book at this time.

Keep reading this book to have a stronger understanding of your identity. Throughout this workbook, you will have lots of opportunities to explore your thoughts and experiences related to your identity and racial stress. You will be guided through activities and discussions to help you practice ways to express your feelings when those difficult moments and intense feelings come up. You may even feel motivated to share your personal experiences with racial stress and trauma with the people in your life who you trust and love. Lastly, we hope that you will have a deeper understanding of racial stress and trauma. And remember, we will be guiding you and coaching you along the way!

As you get started, reflect on the following: What is your earliest memory where you had to deal with something hurtful because of your race?

_____

_____

_____

_____

Do you remember the first time you were aware of your racial identity? Did you become aware of your race because of something someone said or did to you?

_____

_____

_____

_____

What does your racial identity mean to you? This is a place to be honest with yourself about your identity and what your identity means to you. We know that some of your feelings connected to your racial identity may not always be positive, and for now, that is okay. We hope that by starting in an honest place about your feelings and experiences, by the end of your journey through this book, you will be able to feel a greater sense of pride connected to your racial identity.

Let's ponder this question: What does your racial identity mean to you? For example, you might say, "Being Black makes me feel proud and courageous." Or you could think, "Being Black makes me feel different and unaccepted by the world." And still at other times, you might think, "Being Black makes me feel joy." So what would you say?

Being Black makes me feel _____

_____

_____ .

When exploring a difficult experience like racism, it is important to know how frequently it impacts you, so you can come up with the best ways of managing the stress that comes with it. How frequently you experience something like racism can influence how you cope with it.

How much racism do you face in a week? Choose the response that best fits your experiences:

1. Not at all

2. Several days

3. More than half the days

4. Nearly every day

Now that we've talked a little about our goals for you while reading this book, let's explore your goals. What led you to read this book at this moment? Perhaps you recently encountered an act of racism or mistreatment because you are Black. Are you wondering about your identity and what it means to be a Black teen? Maybe you have been watching the news and social media and you want to learn more about social injustices and how this all may be impacting you.

What are the things you want to learn about yourself and your identity from this book? Take a moment to think about it. Just in case it is a challenge for you to identify a goal at this time, we included a few questions to help you to identify some goals.

What goals do you have for understanding your racial identity? Fill in the blanks with what you hope to gain. For example, "I hope to understand how racism affects me."

"I hope to understand myself more." "I hope to learn new ways of dealing with people when I experience any mistreatment because of my race."

At the end of the book, I hope to:

1. _____

2. _____

3. _____

What goals do you have for understanding racial stress and trauma? Fill in the blanks with what you hope to gain. For example, "I hope to feel more comfortable about myself even though I see racism happening in the world." "I hope to better understand how racial stress affects me when it happens to me." "I hope to learn ways to talk to my friends and family about my experiences."

At the end of the book, I hope to:

1. _____

2. _____

3. _____

We know that beginning the journey of understanding racial stress and trauma can sometimes feel heavy. Yet, we also know that you are brave, resilient, and skilled at learning new things. It is our hope not only that you are able to practice and learn the skills presented in this book, but also that you are able to make them your own! We want you to get creative and be honest about your experiences and feelings. Are you ready? We are!

PART 1

Understanding Racism

Racial stress is the emotional and physical response that you might have from a negative racial experience, and it can lead to racial trauma. These experiences tend to have a harmful impact on how you think, feel, and behave. They might occur often or be less frequent. How often you experience racial stress can be related to a lot of different things, like where you live, go to school, and hang out. No matter how often you experience racial stress or racial trauma, it can upset you and cause you to change your views and thoughts about the world and your relationships. So let's look at the different types of racism.

1 name it—what are racism and racial stress?

for you to know

Stress is your emotional and physical response to life events. For example, if you are feeling worried or nervous (emotional response) about an upcoming math test, or if your heart begins to race and your palms begin to sweat (physical response) before you have to give a presentation to your class, you are having emotional and physical responses to stress.

Racial stress refers to the emotional and physical responses that you may have from a negative racial experience. For example, if you have ever been asked to represent your entire race in a class discussion and you feel mad or frustrated, that is an emotional response. Or if you or a member of your family are driving and a police vehicle pulls up behind you, and at that moment, your stomach instantly drops or begins to turn, that is a physical response. These are examples of racial stress and the emotional and physical responses that you may experience in response to a negative racial stressor or encounter.

So you know what racial stress is, but what is *racial trauma*? A racially stressful experience becomes racial trauma if the events cause you emotional and psychological harm that threatens your integrity and safety. Racial trauma refers to the stressful impact or emotional pain of one's experience with racism and discrimination (Carter 2007).

Okay, so now you know a little bit more about stress, racial stress, and racial trauma, but what about all those other terms we mentioned? No worries, we will also describe each of these more specific terms (all related to racial stress) for you in each of the following activities!

for you to do

Let's get started by naming your personal experiences. Place a checkmark beside any of the following experiences if something similar has happened to you.

- ☐ You've scrolled through your Instagram, Snapchat, or TikTok timeline and read comments that used racial slurs or talked negatively about Black people or a group of people because of their race.

- ☐ You've watched a video on YouTube showing the mistreatment of a person of your same racial group, which ultimately ended in that individual being harmed, harassed, or dying.

- ☐ You've been the only person of your racial group in a class discussion related to your racial group. You felt your teacher and peers staring at you, until someone finally directly asked you what your entire race thinks about a particular topic.

- ☐ A peer has asked, "How did you get your hair like that?" while reaching to touch your hair at the same time.

- ☐ Teachers and staff at your school have expected Black students to perform better at sports, with low expectations for academic success.

If you checked any of the statements, you may have experienced a racial stressor. Have you experienced any other situations that you think may also be racial stressors that were not identified above? If so, write them here. As you continue to read through the workbook, you may be able to better understand your experiences and if they may be connected to race.

_____

_____

_____

_____

more to do

We want you to describe what racial stress and racial trauma mean to you. Choose from the chart of experiences, thoughts, and feelings to help you answer the following questions.

Experiences	Thoughts	Feelings
My friend and I both skipped class, but he was allowed to go back to his class. I was suspended for two days. My friend is White and I'm wondering if it's because I'm Black.	I'm alone. No one understands how I feel.	Anger
Being called a racist name while playing an online video game.	This will never get better.	Frustration
Seeing a classmate being teased about the texture/style of her hair.	I'm afraid for my safety.	Sadness
Peers at school commenting on the darkness of my skin tone, in front of other students.	This is unfair.	Anxiety/fear
Feeling afraid when a police officer is behind me while driving.	Why are people so mean?	Blaming myself
Noticing my heart rate increasing when I see videos of police brutality.	I hate racist people.	Humiliation/ embarrassment

You can download a copy of this worksheet at http://www.newharbinger.com/50676 and fill it out as many times as is helpful.

1. What is an example of racial stress and trauma that you may have experienced or that someone you know experienced?

2. If you have experienced racial stress or trauma, what were some of the thoughts you had at the time?

3. If you have experienced racial stress or trauma, how did it make you feel?

Experiences	Thoughts	Feelings

2 when racism is easy to see

for you to know

Overt racist actions are the easiest to see, unlike the less obvious or more hidden forms of racism (known as *covert racism*, which we'll discuss next). "Overt racism or explicit racism is the intentional and/or obvious harmful attitudes or behaviors toward another minority individual or group because of the color of their skin" (Elias 2015). Examples of overt racism can include:

- Hate speech, which is used by individuals to slander, incite hatred, or put down another person or group of people due to their race, skin tone, religion, sexual identity, gender identity, etc.

- Discrimination or treating people differently based on their race

- Racial slurs, like using the word "Darkie" to describe a Black person

- A teacher using the N-word in class

- Hate crimes, which are acts of violence or attacks against a person due to their race (for example, White youth throwing objects at a peer and harming her only because she is Black, or intimidating or harassing youth repeatedly at school only because of their race)

- Racial teasing, which is teasing a student because of their racial features, such as skin tone or hair texture

With the rise of the civil rights movement and passage of civil rights protections in the past fifty years, overt racism has become largely socially unacceptable in American society. However, there has been a rise of overtly racist incidents, such as the rise of reported hate crimes since the election of President Trump (Williamson and Gelfand 2019). Unfortunately, this could mean that a teen like you, or like Alexis (in the following story), could also experience a hate crime or other overt racism.

Alexis is a seventeen-year-old Black girl who lives in a predominantly Black neighborhood and attends her local public high school. She is the middle child. She has an older brother and younger sister. Alexis was a cheerleader for her high school since freshman year but quit the team at the beginning of her senior year so she could watch her younger sister after school. She loves fashion, making TikTok videos, and braiding hair. Alexis recently turned her love for braiding into a business, and braids hair on the weekends to make extra money.

Alexis and her younger sister went shopping at a local haircare store. While they were eager to look at hair-braiding accessories, every time Alexis looked behind her, the saleswoman was following her. Next the saleswoman snapped, "I hate when you people come in here. Whenever we have Black customers, it runs my good customers away." Alexis instantly felt like she had a million butterflies in her stomach, and she suddenly did not feel well. She quickly rushed out of the store.

When Alexis's sister got in the car, she asked Alexis, "What's wrong, why are you sweating like that?" Alexis snapped, "I don't know, I keep replaying what just happened in my mind. Let's just go." Alexis began to feel anxious and felt pressure in her chest. Being in a store where the saleswoman followed her around the store made Alexis feel frustrated and nervous to ever go shopping in that same store again.

for you to do

Now that you have read about Alexis's experience, identify how you think Alexis may have experienced overt racism:

_____

_____

_____

From the list of feelings below, please circle how this experience made Alexis feel:

happy   sad   frustrated   nervous   excited

angry   content   confused   irritable   surprised

What other details in the story do you think are important or give Alexis clues that she is experiencing overt racism?

_____

_____

_____

Questions that may help your reflection: What sensations did Alexis describe feeling in her body? What behaviors and words did the saleswoman use that are suggestive of overt racism?

_____

_____

_____

more to do

Identify examples of overt racism, whether from your life, something you may have witnessed or know others have experienced, or even something you may have seen on the news, and write them in the circles below. You may notice that some experiences occur in multiple circles. For example, an event may have occurred in your own life, and it may have happened to your friend as well. You can write experiences in more than one circle.

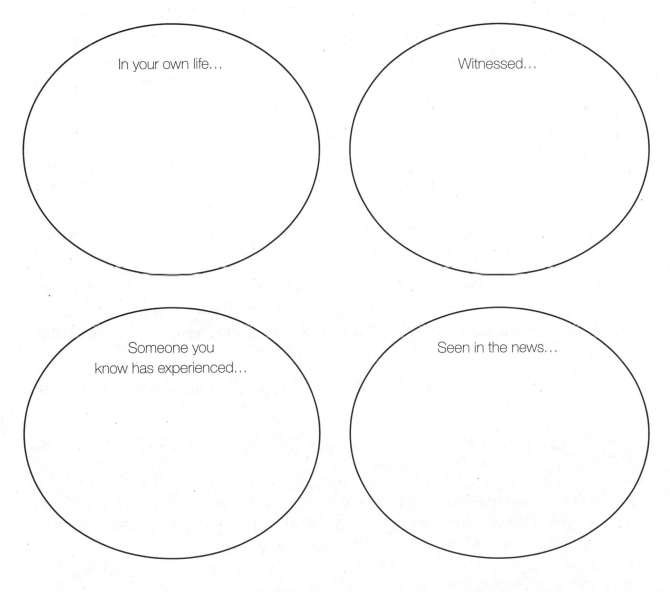

In your own life…

Witnessed…

Someone you
know has experienced…

Seen in the news…

3   when racism is hidden

for you to know

Unlike overt racism, which is more obvious when it occurs, covert racism is not as easy to see or identify when it happens, so it is more difficult to recognize. This is true both for the person performing the racist act and the person on the receiving end of the act. This means that to many people, covert racism is not as obvious—it's more hidden or sneaky, but the impact is still felt in a major way for the individual who is the target of the racist act. Because of the subtle ways that covert racism may occur, it also allows the person committing the act to deny that the behavior or act was racist, leaving you feeling even more hurt and unheard. Examples of covert racism can include:

- Racial profiling—law enforcement or security targeting a person for suspicion of breaking the law only due to their race, including a police officer pulling a Black teenager over while driving for a minor traffic violation (taillight out, dark tinted windows, driving slightly above the speed limit), or a security guard stopping a group of Black teenagers at a mall and ordering to search them for stolen items, without any evidence of them stealing

- Negative stereotypes about a group of people only due to their race, such as "Black teens are more angry or aggressive," "Black students are better athletes than academic performers," or "Black girls are not able to perform well in STEM subjects"

- School policies that unfairly ban students from wearing their hair in its natural state

- A person grabbing their bag or locking their car door when a group of teenagers walk by

- Being invited to attend an event held at your friend's golf club, but upon arriving you are told you cannot enter the golf club due to the way you are dressed, even though your friends are dressed the same way

If you encounter covert racism, you may find yourself replaying the event in your mind after it occurred and questioning yourself or others about if it was in fact racism. This is how covert racism works. Because it is not as obvious as overt racism, which is easy to see, many teens your age may feel confused. This is a common and normal feeling. It is important to remember this, as some teens report feeling "crazy" or they even ask if there is something wrong with them for feeling unsure about the experience. We want you to know that you are *not* "crazy," your experience is real, and these are normal feelings and reactions to covert racism.

for you to do

Myka is a seventeen-year-old Black girl who lives in a mostly Black neighborhood. One Saturday morning, Myka drove her younger brother to his math tutoring session in a close by, predominantly White suburb. While Myka waited for her brother to finish with tutoring, she ran errands in the neighborhood. There was a video game store she was excited about checking out to see what exciting new games were coming out.

Myka arrived at the store, parked her mom's truck, and rushed in. Myka greeted the employee by saying, "Hello. How are you? I am so happy to hear about the new released games!"

The employee gave Myka a slight smile and softly replied, "Hello. Are you in the right place, sweetie?"

Myka then heard another employee loudly whisper, "Too bad she cannot afford those new games."

Myka cringed. She instantly felt embarrassed, annoyed, and mad. She thought to herself, How does she know what I can afford? *However, determined to not let the store employees dim her excitement, she found the games she was looking for and went to check out.*

Thinking about Myka, how do you think she may have experienced covert racism? Include any details you think are important.

_____

_____

_____

_____

_____

_____

more to do

Have you experienced covert racism before? If so, use the chart of experiences, thoughts, and feelings to help you answer the following questions. You can also download a copy of this worksheet at http://www.newharbinger.com/50676.

1. What is an example of covert racism that you may have experienced or that someone you know experienced?

2. If you have experienced covert racism, what were some of the thoughts you had at the time?

3. If you have experienced covert racism, how did it make you feel?

Experiences	Thoughts	Feelings

4 when you are unsure it is racism

for you to know

Microaggressions can occur as a verbal comment that feels hurtful or insulting, such as an offensive racial term aimed at a person due to their race, someone touching a Black girl's hair without permission because the texture is different from theirs, or as all the images in a school being of White people and not representing its Black students.

All of these examples of microaggressions may lead to you feeling hurt, invalidated, or unseen, and may also make you feel different and as if you don't belong in that environment. Many teens your age report experiencing microaggressions daily. Microaggressions can show up in so many different ways, including verbal statements (something offensive or hurtful that someone may say to you), behaviors (something someone may do toward you), and environmental (lack of representation in an environment or rules that are offensive and not inclusive of the experience of Black people).

Although microaggressions may not always appear intentional, they are hurtful and can have a negative impact on how you feel. Examples of microaggressions can include:

- Teachers continually mispronouncing Black students' names

- Teachers complimenting Black students on their use of "good English" or stating, "You are so articulate"

- Someone saying, "You're pretty for a Black girl," or "You're pretty for a dark-skinned girl," as a compliment

- Educators perceiving the same behaviors (e.g., advocating for student rights in a school) as being more aggressive or hostile when they're done by a Black student

- Administrators spending more time watching the behavior of students of color in the hallways, at recess, or in the cafeteria due to the misperception that they are more likely to break a school rule

- People asking you where you are from or "what are you mixed with" due to your physical characteristics (skin complexion, hair type), assuming that you are not Black or that Black people are not dynamic and do not appear in a range of complexions and physical features

It is important to remember that although a microaggression may appear like a small, minimal, or overlooked act in the moment or environment, the impact of a single microaggression, and the compounded impact of microaggressions over time, are hurtful and can have a huge impact on you and how you feel.

for you to do

Madison is a sixteen-year-old Black girl. She recently made the cheer team and has become close friends with another teammate, Maggie. Maggie is a fifteen-year-old White girl who just moved to town. Madison and Maggie went shopping at the local mall to find hair accessories to match their new cheer uniforms. While shopping, Madison found hair bows and excitedly shared them with Maggie. Maggie loved the bows! She took one, and while trying one on she replied, "These are perfect for my hair because my hair is so silky and straight. Your hair is way too thick and nappy for these bows; they would not look good on you."

Reflect on this story with Madison. What microaggression did Madison experience?

_____

_____

What feelings do you think Madison may have felt?

_____

_____

_____

What are some ways that Madison could respond to Maggie?

_____

_____

_____

_____

_____

You can also use this chart of experiences, thoughts, and feelings to help you better understand Madison's experience of a microaggression and what she may have thought and felt as a result. A copy of this worksheet is available at http://www.newharbinger .com/50676.

Experiences	Thoughts	Feelings

more to do

As previously mentioned, many teens your age have experienced microaggressions, sometimes daily. Take a few moments to reflect on your experiences at school, with peers, on social media, or even while gaming online. Write a list of the microaggressions that you have encountered.

_____

_____

_____

_____

Identify an example or multiple microaggressions from your list above and write a reflective journal entry about the feelings you experienced.

Here are some example sentences to get you started on your journal entry: "I felt _____ when _____. This experience made me feel _____ because _____. I know this experience is an example of a microaggression because _____."

_____

_____

_____

_____

_____

_____

_____

stereotypes that lead to racism $\qquad$ 5

for you to know

Ever since she could remember, Lauren has wanted to be a scientist. She loved doing science experiments in class as a young child; she attended summer camps that focused on science and learning; she excelled in all of her science classes through high school, including AP Physics; and last summer she was invited to spend a week at a NASA-sponsored summer camp. So when it was time to apply for colleges, there was no doubt that Lauren was going to major in an area of science. For Lauren that major was chemistry, and she was determined to apply to a historically Black college or university (HBCU).

Whenever Lauren shared her goal major and college dreams with others, she noticed that people had very different comments and reactions. Her family was extremely proud, as Lauren, a seventeen-year-old Black girl, was going to be the first person in her family to attend and graduate from college. But everyone else had different responses:

- *Lauren noticed that her counselor often made comments such as, "You're so bright. Are you sure you don't want to add other types of schools to your list?" or "If you attend an HBCU, you may not be able to achieve your career goals."*

- *Her friends would make comments such as, "Why are you applying to those schools? We haven't even heard of them."*

- *And every once in a while, a teacher or adult would suggest she change her major to something like dance or psychology, saying, "Science may be too hard for you."*

Lauren heard all the comments. She could feel that some people didn't agree with her school choices or her major, and although she was more determined than ever to follow through with her plans, Lauren felt hurt and down and she couldn't figure out why.

Lauren's experiences—the teachers' reactions to her major, her counselor suggesting that she should apply to different types of schools because attending an HBCU will not prepare her for her career choice, and her friends making comments about her school selections—are behaviors known as *implicit biases*.

Implicit biases are attitudes and beliefs that affect our behaviors. We are not always consciously aware they exist, but they do. They are biases that are sometimes automatic and can include racial stereotypes, such as, "Attending a predominantly white college is the only way to succeed," or "Science may be too hard for Lauren." Although these biases can show up in small interactions between two people, they can also show up in larger systems, such as the legal system, college admissions, or even hiring practices, and have the ability to negatively impact our larger society. Implicit bias doesn't feel good to the person on the receiving end of it and may explain why Lauren was feeling hurt and down. Implicit bias can also:

- Be so subtle that it is not noticeable at first, and you might even be confused about whether it occurred or if you should have an emotional response to it

- Be expressed in subconscious stereotypes (automatic responses you may have without thinking about them)

- Impact our expectations and interactions with people

- Include judgments based on race, ability, gender, culture, language, etc.

- Impact how teachers perceive and respond to students

Examples of implicit bias can include:

- Holding an implicit stereotype that labels Black people as violent or more aggressive, and as a result, a person may cross the street at night when they see a Black man walking in their direction, without even realizing why they are crossing the street

- In the school setting, a teacher holding an implicit stereotype that all Black males are good at sports, and as a result, suggesting that Black male students should focus more energy on sports than academics

- A teacher complimenting a Black Latino student for speaking perfect English, but he is actually a native English speaker—the teacher assumed that simply because the student is Latino, English would not be his first language

for you to do

What are some examples of implicit biases that you have experienced?

_____

_____

_____

How did you feel when you experienced implicit bias?

_____

_____

_____

How did you respond to the implicit bias?

_____

_____

_____

How would you like to respond in the future?

_____

_____

_____

more to do

Use this space to name or draw reminders to yourself that you and your future are not defined by other people's stereotypes or implicit biases. This is a space to remind yourself that, even when it doesn't feel good, you have the capability to push through and keep going. In this space, you can write more affirmations to yourself ("I am deserving of a future not defined by the world"), draw a picture that represents your hopes for the future and changes you hope to see related to Black people in America, identify places where you feel safe to be yourself or where you feel most understood, or even write motivational words that you can reread when you are having a tough moment. You can also draw images that are significant to you.

when you see other people experience racism

for you to know

You can hear about or observe acts of racism or discrimination toward other people on social media or the news, or hear a friend speak about an experience of racism. This is *indirect* or *vicarious* exposure to racism. Someone else's experiences may lead to an emotional or physical response from you. Examples of vicarious experiences with racial stress can include:

- Viewing the killing of unarmed Black and Brown people by police on television or the internet

- Witnessing someone being teased due to their race (physical characteristics, hair type, speech or language, skin complexion) on social media

- Hearing about attempts by someone of a different race to hurt or murder others from your racial background

- Persistent racial bullying (e.g., students in your school targeting and bullying another student only due to that student being Black) or witnessing someone else of your same racial group being described by others using derogatory language (e.g., "big nose," comparisons to an animal to describe features)

for you to do

Ian, a thirteen-year-old boy, loves playing video games. He regularly checks YouTube to learn new strategies to advance levels on his games. One day while watching a video, he started to scroll through the comment section. One comment really stood out to him, instantly made him feel hot all over his body, and caused him to begin to breathe heavily. Ian realized that the person who made the comment is also a friend from his school. The commenter used an ugly racial slur directed at another viewer and stated that anyone with a White dad and Black mom "does not belong anywhere." Ian is biracial. He has a White dad and Black mom, and at times struggles with fitting in with his peers.

Based on Ian's story, what vicarious experience or racial stress did he encounter? What other details in the story do you think are important or give Ian clues that he was experiencing vicarious racism?

_____

_____

_____

_____

Questions that may help your reflection: What sensations did Ian describe feeling in his body? What do you think Ian was feeling about his friend being the person who wrote the comment?

_____

_____

_____

_____

more to do

Much like Ian, oftentimes when teens experience a vicarious trauma, they may also have a physical reaction in their body, such as "hot all over his body, and caused him to begin to breathe heavily." It is important to understand how your body responds to racial stress and trauma so that you can better understand your feelings and emotions, and to identify strategies that may be most helpful for you to deal with the stress. If you have experienced a vicarious trauma, label the feelings you experienced after the trauma and where you felt them in your body in the below image. To label the feelings you had in your body for more than one experience, you can download a copy of this worksheet at http://www.newharbinger.com/50676.

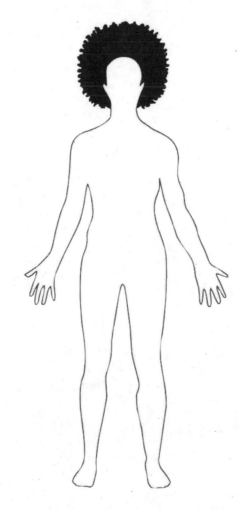

7 when you experience racism

for you to know

Let's reflect. Name your experiences. Now that we have defined various types of racial stress, reflect on your personal encounters with it. Recall a direct (it happened to you) or indirect (it happened to someone else) experience of racial stress and respond to the following questions. To answer the questions for more experiences, you can download a copy of this worksheet at http://www.newharbinger.com/50676 and fill it out as many times as is helpful.

for you to do

Name the experience: _____

What type of racial stressor(s) did you experience? Use the definitions we shared.	
Did you recognize it as a racial stressor when it first occurred?	
Where were you?	
When did it occur?	
What emotions did you feel?	
What physical response(s) did you experience— did your body react?	
Who did you share your experience with?	
What questions are you left with right now?	

more to do

You identified trusted adults and family members as you began this workbook. Do you feel comfortable reaching out to them when you need to share your feelings about racial stress?

One way to initiate that conversation is to open up with them about this workbook that you are reading and even to request an interview. These are great ways to initiate discussions around racial stress, by allowing the trusted adults in your life to tell you about their personal experiences and feelings connected to racial stress. In some ways, learning about a trusted adult's experiences may help you to build connections to others as you learn more about your own experiences.

First, identify a trusted adult you would like to interview and write that person's name here: _____

Next, ask the following questions and write down their responses.

What is your first memory of being Black?

_____

_____

_____

_____

What types of experiences with racial stress did you experience at my age?

_____

_____

_____

_____

How did you deal with the racial stress you experienced when you were my age?

_____

_____

_____

Have you experienced racial stress as an adult? How does it make you feel now?

_____

_____

_____

What new strategies have you found helpful as an adult to deal with racial stressors?

_____

_____

_____

What does your identity mean to you even though you've experienced racial stress?

_____

_____

_____

What advice would you give me as a teen about how to manage racial stress?

_____

_____

_____

What additional questions do you want to ask? Use this space to write your own questions and responses.

Additional Question 1: _____

_____

_____

_____

Additional Question 2: _____

_____

_____

_____

Additional Question 3: _____

_____

_____

_____

If you are not able to identify some racial experiences, that is okay. Just note that this book will help you gain clarity as you move forward. We will continue to explore these stressors throughout the book and give you strategies to identify your thoughts, feelings, and behaviors, so you can apply strategies to manage how you feel.

PART 2

Exploring How Racial Stress Can Impact You

While we may not be able to change how often you experience racial stress, we would like to help you become much more aware of how these experiences impact the way you think, feel, and act. The first step is to practice identifying thoughts, feelings, and behaviors. Remember, in order to improve and change the choices that you make, you must first understand how these situations impact the way you think and feel. As you read further in the book, you will also learn how to deal with those difficult thoughts and feelings.

8 who am I?

for you to know

One important part of your identity that we will talk about in this chapter is your race and racial identity. Our thoughts and attitudes about the racial group that we belong to have a big impact on our racial identity. However, it is important to remember that not everyone is in the same place on their racial identity journey. Some people are very aware of their race and other people don't even think of their race as an important part of their identity.

The way that you think about yourself as a member of your race and the way you think others perceive you as a member of your race are both important parts of your racial identity (Seaton, Scottham, and Sellers 2006). Your racial identity changes as you have different experiences and learn more about yourself and other people. The way you think about race and your racial identity now can be different than what you think two weeks from now, or even two years from now.

Dante is a fifteen-year-old Black boy who lives in a predominantly Black neighborhood. He has a younger brother, loves hip hop music, and is on the school chess team. Dante attends a charter school in a neighborhood across town, and he is usually the only Black person in most of his classes. Attending a predominantly White school has been difficult for Dante because he's had some negative experiences and often feels like he does not fit in. For example, Dante has been on the chess team for two years, but still remembers when he walked into the first chess team meeting and one of the students said, "The basketball team meeting is in the room down the hall." After he made the chess team and told one of his teachers, his teacher said, "Really? I didn't expect someone like you to enjoy playing chess." Hearing biased comments like this made Dante think a lot more about his race and how the White students and teachers thought about him. As a result of his experiences, Dante also wanted to learn more about Black history and the accomplishments of his ancestors, so he started reading more and talking to his parents about Black history. Dante realized that the more that he learned, the prouder he became of his race. He also found out that there were other famous Black chess players, and he was excited to be standing on the shoulders of giants who shared his heritage!

for you to do

Take a moment and think about how you would describe yourself to someone who does not know you. You might describe yourself by activities you participate in or like to do, like cook, or you might describe yourself by certain characteristics, like if you are a boy or girl, brother or sister, middle or high school student. When you think about who you are, what comes to mind? List below the different ways that you describe yourself:

1. _____

2. _____

3. _____

4. _____

5. _____

6. _____

7. _____

8. _____

Now consider how important race is to you when you think about your identity. Select a number on the scale below that best describes how important your race is to your identity.

Not Important	A Little	I'm Not Sure	Important	Very Important
1	2	3	4	5

Write down why you selected that number:

_____

_____

_____

_____

_____

Now we want you to think a little harder about what your race means to you, and in this next exercise use the blank page to draw or create a collage by cutting out pictures from your favorite magazines. You can find and use pictures, words, or symbols that are important to you and your race. For example, if "proud," "intelligent," or "inventor" are words that you think about, then we want you to include them. If eating soul food and cooking are important, add something that represents those activities. Remember, you can draw, write, or even cut pictures or words out of a magazine. We want you to be creative in this exercise when expressing what your race means to you, so you choose. You will do great. Take your time!

more to do

How you feel about your race may have to do with how you first learned about race and how you were treated because of your race.

How do you feel about your race?

_____

_____

_____

When did you first become aware of your race?

_____

_____

_____

What did your parents or other important adults in your life discuss with you about race?

_____

_____

_____

Did you have a positive or negative racial experience that made you more aware of your race?

_____

_____

_____

Some people did not have discussions with their parents or other important adults about their race. It is important to remember that everyone's experience is different. Now that you've learned about racial identity and completed a few activities to better understand what your race means to you, how you learned about race, and how your experiences with race have impacted you, it is time for you to learn about how your race and experiences with your race impact how you think.

9 identify your thoughts

for you to know

Our thoughts are often related to what we are experiencing in the moment. For example, watching the traumatic killing of a Black person on social media can cause our mind to have thoughts like *This keeps happening to us, They are killing us, We don't deserve this, It can happen to me,* or *I hate the police.* Experiencing these types of thoughts over and over again can lead to high levels of racial stress. In the activities in this section, you will have a chance to explore how your thoughts have been or could be impacted by racially stressful situations.

One day, Jawan was walking to the store with three of his friends to get some snacks. The store that they were walking to had been robbed a few times before. When the store owner was on the news, he made some negative comments about Black people. As Jawan and his friends got closer to the store, he began to think about how the store owner might respond when they walked in. Jawan wondered if the owner might think they were coming to rob the store, or if the store owner might say something to them. He started to think about whether it would be better for him and his friends to go into the store one at a time, or if they should even go in at all. Jawan had so many thoughts going through his head at the same time that he couldn't decide what to do.

for you to do

List at least five events that led to high levels of racial stress that may have caused you to feel scared, angry, helpless, or frustrated.

1. _____

2. _____

3. _____

4. _____

5. _____

List at least five events that have made you feel empowered, happy, hopeful, or proud of your race.

1. _____

2. _____

3. _____

4. _____

5. _____

more to do

Now that you have identified some events that brought up some strong emotions for you, in this next section we will explore the thoughts you had about those events. Go back and look at the two lists you created in the last activity. We would like you to identify four of the experiences you wrote about and describe the thoughts you had during those experiences. Pay close attention to how your thoughts may have changed based on the specific experience. We provided two examples for you below.

Experience	Thoughts
Pulled over by the police.	Will I be killed too? The police are racist.
Learning about Black inventors and how they contributed greatly to the American culture.	We can do great things. We changed the world.

Did your thoughts change based on the experiences?   Yes   No

Which experiences led to more empowering thoughts?

_____

_____

_____

Which experiences led to more distressing or less helpful thoughts?

_____

_____

_____

Describe any changes in emotion or any changes in your body you noticed as you were writing about your experiences and thoughts.

_____

_____

_____

_____

Remember, our thoughts are very powerful and can impact how we feel and what we do. Luckily, our thoughts are one of the things we can control when we are in stressful situations. You'll get some more practice with this in the next section.

even more to do

Sometimes the thoughts that we have about events may not be helpful, but sometimes our thoughts can be empowering. For example, after seeing the way that Black people are treated by the police, you might think, *I'm going to make a change in my community when I get older by becoming a mayor,* or *I'm going to study law when I go to college so I can work on changing things.*

We want you to complete the sentences below by identifying empowering and positive thoughts that may be helpful to you and others after experiencing a negative situation. We know this may be hard and challenging, but you can do it! Remember, we cannot control how people react to us, but we can control how we think and react to them.

Example: The other kids called me dumb because I am Black, but I know *I can achieve anything I put my mind to.*

Now you try! Remember, finish the sentence with empowering and positive thoughts.

1. I know that I may one day get pulled over by the police, but I will remember

   _____

2. My friend's mom told her she was not allowed to hang around me because I am Black, but

   _____

3. My teacher told me that she did not think I would be able to go to college, but

   _____

4. If I see my friend being harassed by the police, I will

   _____

5. When I start to feel down and upset, I will remind myself

   _____

How do you feel after creating those empowering thoughts? We know it's not always easy to come up with empowering or positive thoughts when you are in a stressful situation. Sometimes our minds freeze up and we can't think at all when we are really stressed or scared. Some people find it helpful to remind themselves of empowering or positive thoughts when they start their day or when they are feeling calm.

Is there something you tell yourself when you are starting to get stressed out or you just want to remind yourself of how awesome you are? If you can't think of anything, check out the list below and circle one message that you like. Try saving the message on your phone or computer, or write it on a piece of paper and stick it on the mirror. It doesn't matter where you put it. Just put it somewhere you will see it every day!

EMPOWERING & POSITIVE THOUGHTS:
I was created to change the world!
I am beautiful, brave, and brilliant!
I accept and love everything about myself.
I am in control of my destiny.
I am worthy of respect and love.

Did any of those thoughts sound like something you would say to yourself every day? If not, create one that works for you below:

_____

_____

_____

_____

You are awesome! You have been working really hard and spending a lot of time thinking about some things that are really difficult. We spent a lot of time focusing on thoughts in this section. Sometimes the thoughts that bother us the most tend to come back over and over again. One way to help with that is to make sure you also spend time focusing on empowering and helpful thoughts. The thoughts that we give most of our attention to have the biggest impact on our feelings and behaviors, which is why it is so important to examine them. If you would like to get some more practice identifying the experiences, thoughts, and feelings you have about various situations, you can download a copy of the Experiences, Thoughts, and Feelings worksheet at http://www.newharbinger.com/50676.

We've already looked at how racial stress can impact our behaviors and thoughts. In the next section, we will take a closer look at how racial stress can impact our feelings.

for you to know

Our thoughts are often related to how we are feeling in the moment. Feelings are the emotions that we experience. Our emotions can let us know how we are affected by a specific event. There are not any good or bad feelings because all feelings are important and valid. You can also experience many different emotions at the same time. For example, if someone at school said something racist to you and got suspended, you might feel happy that they got in trouble but also worried that it might happen again.

When you experience racial stress, you may also have a lot of different feelings come up. When you have a lot of different feelings at once, it can be hard to identify them, understand them, or talk about them. In this section, you will have a chance to think more about your feelings and how they are changed by your thoughts and experiences.

Over the past few years, Nikita's parents have talked with her about being careful with police officers, and how to interact with law enforcement if she is ever detained, arrested, or pulled over while driving. While Nikita always listened to her parents when they talked to her about issues about race and law enforcement, she never thought she would have any run-ins with the police. Today, while watching some funny videos on her phone, Nikita clicked on a recent video that went viral, which showed a clip of a Black girl, in her neighborhood, getting beat up by police officers during an arrest. She started wondering about whether something like that would ever happen to her and she started to feel scared, angry, and sad.

for you to do

After reading that story about Nikita, what feelings came up for you? Maybe it reminded you of something that you or your friends have experienced, or made you think about something you saw on the news. Did it cause you to think about something someone in your family told you about the police? Thinking about events like this can be pretty overwhelming. Take a minute and check in with yourself. Look at the list of feelings below and circle all the feelings that describe how you are feeling right now. To identify your feelings in the future, you can download a copy of this worksheet at http://www. newharbinger.com/50676 and fill it out as many times as is helpful.

SAD	CONFUSED	MAD	SCARED	ENERGIZED	CALM
ashamed	dazed	agitated	anxious	challenged	comfortable
crushed	doubtful	angry	concerned	determined	content
depressed	embarrassed	annoyed	helpless	eager	grateful
disappointed	helpless	disgusted	insecure	enthusiastic	peaceful
guilty	lost	furious	nervous	focused	reflective
hurt	shocked	hateful	stressed	hopeful	relaxed
inferior	stuck	irritated	terrified	inspired	thankful
pessimistic	surprised	outraged	uneasy	motivated	thoughtful
unhappy	uncertain	upset	worried	optimistic	undisturbed

more to do

Imagine that you are talking in class to one of your friends and your teacher tells you to stop being so disruptive. A few minutes later, you notice that a White student is talking to one of her friends and the teacher doesn't say anything. You think, *Why did the teacher ask me to stop talking and not the White student?* Let's explore your feelings about this situation.

List your feelings: _____

_____

_____

_____

even more to do

In this exercise, we want you to think about the different types of racism that you learned in part 1 of this book. Sometimes people are racist in their thoughts, actions, or both. Sometimes racism may be harder or easier for us to recognize. This exercise will focus on some of these different types of racism. We want you to think about racially stressful or traumatic situations that you experienced over the past year. After you identify these situations, we want you to identify the thoughts and feelings you had about them.

Remember, overt racism is an obvious and harmful attitude or behavior toward another individual or group because of the color of their skin. It could be a situation that happened directly to you—meaning you, personally, felt discriminated against or treated unfairly because of your race or background. For example, you may have experienced a situation where someone accused you of stealing because you are Black, saying, "I know you stole it. Black people steal." In that situation, it is obvious, which makes it overt racism.

Now you identify an overt racism situation that you experienced:

_____

Thoughts	Feelings

Remember, microaggressions are more subtle, daily encounters that are harmful, but not as obvious as overt racism. Some examples may be a teacher continually mispronouncing Black students' names or someone saying, "You're pretty for a Black girl."

Now you identify a microaggression situation that you experienced:

_____

Thoughts	Feelings

Remember indirect or vicarious exposure to racism is hearing about or seeing others experience racism or discrimination. It can be a situation that you heard about or witnessed in your community, on social media, or online. For example, while walking home from school, you saw a Black girl being arrested after she was attacked by a group of White girls. She was the only one arrested and the police assumed she started the fight. Another example may be your watching a YouTube video of a Black man being shot and killed by the police.

Now you identify an indirect or vicarious exposure to racism situation that you experienced:

_____

Thoughts	Feelings

You are doing great! You just learned that your experiences with your race can impact how you feel. You also got a chance to think about past situations that impacted how you think and feel. If you thought of other situations that you would like to explore your thoughts and feelings about or you want to complete this exercise again, you can download the Experiences, Thoughts, and Feelings worksheet at http://www .newharbinger.com/50676. In the next activity, you will get a chance to learn how other experiences with race may influence or change your behavior.

11 understand your behaviors

for you to know

Behaviors are specific actions that we engage in. Sometimes you make choices about how to behave based on the thoughts or feelings you are experiencing at that time. Sometimes our brain does things so quickly we aren't even aware of it.

When you experience racial stress, you may also knowingly or unknowingly make certain choices as a result of that experience. For example, when you experience racial stress, you might cry, want to be alone, yell, or scream. On the other hand, you might speak out more about racism, journal about your experiences, or become more active and involved in your community.

In this section, you will have an opportunity to explore how your thoughts and feelings about racial stress impact your behaviors. With practice you can learn how to make smart choices even when you are feeling upset or experiencing negative thoughts. Practicing the exercises in this chapter is a great way to start working on it! Remember, we must first be aware of our actions before we can change them.

After school Chase and her girlfriend, Nyla, went to the mall with their friend Shawn. While shopping for new school shoes, they noticed that they were being followed in the store by the White store manager. The manager said, "If you all aren't going to buy anything, please leave." Chase got really upset and said she wanted to punch the manager in his face. Nyla and Shawn couldn't believe what they heard! They felt shocked and frustrated and walked out of the store.

Later, while they were sitting in the food court, Nyla said, "I hate that people think that just because we are young and Black, that we don't have money. All of us have jobs and work hard for what we have. We don't do anything different than the other White teenagers who shop at the mall, but we are the ones who are always getting harassed." Shawn started talking about all the smart and successful Black teenagers that they know and how one of their best friends just received a $50,000 scholarship for college. Chase, Nyla, and Shawn started to discuss what they were going to do after they graduate from high school. They all had plans to be successful and agreed that they weren't going to let anyone or anything stand in their way.

for you to do

Unfortunately, what happened to Chase happens to a lot of people. When things like that happen, it can be difficult to know exactly how to respond. You might feel so angry that it feels like you are going to explode and you may want to tell everyone about your experience. You might feel so shocked and embarrassed that you can barely speak. There is no right or wrong way to feel in a situation like this. The important thing to remember is that all of your emotions, no matter what they are, are important and valid. In this next section, you will have a chance to think more about what you might do if something like this happens to you.

Imagine you are shopping with your friend at the mall. Your friend picks up a cute sweater and starts heading your way to show it to you. As she approaches you, you notice that a White salesperson quickly steps in front of her and asks her where she is taking the sweater. Your friend informs the salesperson that she was coming to show it to you. The salesperson steps aside and rolls her eyes. Then you overhear the salesperson say to someone else who is working in the store, "Those kind of people are always stealing from our store. We have to keep a close eye on them."

Have you experienced a situation like this before? Or maybe even heard about it happening to someone else? An experience like that could bring up a lot of different thoughts and feelings for you and for your friend.

Let's start with your thoughts. What sort of thoughts came up for you as you were reading this scenario? Let's try something a little different here. Set a timer for five minutes and write down every single thought that comes to mind about that experience of shopping at the mall. There are no right or wrong thoughts. There is no right or wrong way to feel. This is just an opportunity for you to get all those thoughts out of your head and onto paper. Are you ready? Set your timer. And go!

_____

_____

_____

_____

_____

_____

_____

_____

Time is up! How was that? Was it hard to get started? Hard to stop? Spending time with our thoughts can sometimes be difficult, especially if we are thinking about an unpleasant situation. But sometimes, after spending time with our thoughts, our minds feel a little less foggy and we feel a little better.

Thinking about that experience of racial profiling at the store could have brought up a lot of different feelings for you. After an exercise like that, it is important to take a minute and check in with yourself to see how you are feeling. Take a look at the following feelings chart and circle the top five feelings that you are experiencing right now. You can also download a copy of this worksheet at http://www.newharbinger .com/50676 and fill it out as many times as is helpful.

SAD	CONFUSED	MAD	SCARED	ENERGIZED	CALM
ashamed	dazed	agitated	anxious	challenged	comfortable
crushed	doubtful	angry	concerned	determined	content
depressed	embarrassed	annoyed	helpless	eager	grateful
disappointed	helpless	disgusted	insecure	enthusiastic	peaceful
guilty	lost	furious	nervous	focused	reflective
hurt	shocked	hateful	stressed	hopeful	relaxed
inferior	stuck	irritated	terrified	inspired	thankful
pessimistic	surprised	outraged	uneasy	motivated	thoughtful
unhappy	uncertain	upset	worried	optimistic	undisturbed

Now that you have had an opportunity to express your thoughts and reflect on your feelings, let's think about your behaviors. How would you respond to a situation like this?

What would you say to your friend?

_____

_____

Would you say anything to the salesperson or anyone else at the store? Why or why not?

_____

_____

Would you talk to anyone at home about what happened? Why or why not?

_____

_____

What would you do after you got home?

_____

_____

Do you think you would go back to that store again?

_____

_____

Sometimes it can be helpful to think about situations that could happen in the future so that we can come up with a plan. Having a plan can help us feel less anxious and more prepared when unexpected situations arise. You were asked to do a lot of reflection in this section. If you weren't sure about how you would handle a situation where you were discriminated against in a store and you need some more time to think about it, you can always come back to this section when you are ready.

more to do

There are probably a lot of situations involving race at school, in your community, and even on TV, that you have seen or experienced that caused you to have a lot of different thoughts and feelings. In this next exercise, we would like you to identify what thoughts, feelings, and behaviors someone your age might have if they experienced a racially stressful or traumatic situation. We have provided a chart with several examples of thoughts, feelings, and behaviors below. As you review the list, circle any thoughts, feelings, or behaviors that you have experienced as a result of a stressful or traumatic situation involving your race.

Thoughts	Feelings	Behaviors
My teacher is racist.	Angry	I stopped asking my teacher for help.
The students at my school hate me because I am Black.	Worthless	I skip school.
The police kill Black people.	Scared	Try to hide if I see the police.
When I walk down the street no one looks at me.	Invisible	I don't speak to anyone.
My mom worries about me whenever I leave the house.	Overwhelmed	Text my mom when I get where I am going.
It seems hard for White people to trust me.	Frustrated	Avoid White people.
I wonder if I will still be alive when my little sister graduates.	Powerless	Listen to my music.
There is too much hate in this world.	Upset	Join a peace rally.

There are so many different ways that you might think, feel, or respond after experiencing a racially stressful situation. You might have circled a few things in the previous examples, or maybe none at all. Either way, it's okay. We're going to give you a chance now to come up with your own examples.

Take a few minutes and think about what else you might add to the list, and see if you can fill in the second chart below. Think about racially stressful or traumatic experiences you have had that resulted in certain thoughts and behaviors and fill in the chart below. To explore your thoughts, feelings, and behaviors in the future, you can download a copy of this worksheet at http://www.newharbinger.com/50676 and fill it out as many times as is helpful.

Thoughts	Feelings	Behaviors

Thinking about racially stressful situations like that can be difficult. Take a minute and check in with yourself to see how you are feeling. When you are ready, you can move on to the next exercise.

In this next exercise, we would like you to identify what thoughts, feelings, and behaviors you might have if you experienced a positive situation where you felt empowered, happy, hopeful, or proud of your race. We have provided a chart with several examples for you. Take a few minutes to review the chart below. Then you'll have a chance to create your own list.

Thoughts	Feelings	Behaviors
I love learning about my culture.	Proud	Told my parents what I learned.
Justice was served.	Hopeful	Smiled.
Change can be made.	Empowered	Read about law school and how I can make a difference.
We have accomplished great things.	Excited	Applied for college.
I can create change.	Worthy	Joined community organization/club.
They are honoring us.	Uplifted	Smiled.
Our Black-student-led organization was acknowledged by the principal.	Valued	Created more activities in the community.
They thanked us.	Appreciated	Told family and friends that we were acknowledged.

There are so many different ways that you might think, feel, or respond after experiencing a positive situation where you felt empowered, happy, hopeful, or proud of your race. We're going to give you a chance now to come up with your own examples. Take a few minutes, think about what else you might add to the list, and see if you can fill in the chart below. Think about positive experiences you have had and add your thoughts, feelings, and behaviors in the chart below.

Thoughts	Feelings	Behaviors

What did you notice when doing this exercise?

_____

_____

_____

Are there certain thoughts or feelings that you would like to experience more or less of?

_____

_____

_____

What behaviors are most helpful when you experience racial stress?

_____

_____

_____

Perhaps filling out these charts made you think about someone you know or have heard about. It is not often that we stop to ask ourselves about our experiences with racism or racial stress. It can be helpful to think about how racism impacts us because the first step in healing and creating change is understanding. It may not have been easy for you to identify your thoughts, feelings, and behaviors. The more you practice, the easier it gets!

12 see the impact on your relationships

for you to know

Healthy relationships are important because they can help us manage stress and can be a source of support and strength. Healthy relationships can also give us a sense of purpose, help us grow, and make us feel happy. When you go through ups and downs in life, the people who you have healthy relationships with can cheer you on and support you.

You may notice that racial stress and trauma can impact your feelings of trust and safety in your relationships with important people in your life, such as your parents, siblings, friends, teachers, and coaches. For example, if you experience racial teasing on social media, it is normal to feel vulnerable or confused about who your "safe people" really are. Experiences with racial stress and trauma may make you worry not just about yourself but also about the safety of others in your life. These worries can sometimes lead you to feel like you have to constantly be on guard or ready to defend yourself in a racist situation, which can make you feel lonely, furious, and suspicious of other people.

You may also notice that changes in your mood and thoughts—like feeling more angry or worried than usual—can influence your relationships. These feelings can feel overwhelming, and later in this book we will share ways to help you manage these big emotions. For now, let's look at how racial stress impacts your relationships.

for you to do

Each race-based experience is different. There are a few important things to think about when understanding how and if racial stress and trauma impact your relationships. Let's consider the following example.

Dallas is a fourteen-year-old boy who is very involved at school and in his community. While at a basketball game, Dallas bumped into older students from his school that he did not know very well. He recognized one of the boys, Adam, from the football team that he played on last summer. He remembered that Adam sometimes bullied younger kids from school.

As Dallas passed by the group of boys, he heard Adam yell, "You better hurry up and get home so you don't disappear when the sun goes down!"

The group of boys started laughing, and Dallas overheard another boy, Kevin, say, "You need to stop talking trash about people's dark skin. Isn't your mom that color? And also dark skin is beautiful, man."

Dallas ignored the boys and walked home quickly. He noticed his heart racing, hands sweating, and tears starting to form in his eyes. When he walked in the house, he slammed the door, ignored his father and little brother who were in the living room, and walked up to his room. His little brother asked, "What's wrong with you?"

Dallas yelled, "Nothing, stupid, leave me alone!"

Let's use the three-step relationship reflection process (describe, assess, reflect) to describe what happened in this situation, assess the level of stress, and reflect on how the stressor influenced Dallas's relationships and reactions. We will also think about if there was anything that could have been done to ask for support or attempt to repair each relationship.

Step 1: *Describe* the situation. Now that we know what happened, reflect on the details of the experience (who, when, where, why) and the details that alerted you to see that the situation was related to racism or racial stress.

Who: _____

When: _____

Where: _____

Why: _____

Step 2: *Assess* the racial stress level. Reflect on how stressful you think the situation was for Dallas and the details that were signs of stress.

On a scale of 1 to 10, with 1 being no stress and 10 being extreme stress, rate how stressful the event was: _____

What details (thoughts, feelings, behaviors) were signs of stress? _____

_____

What percentage do you think was general relationship stress and how much do you think was specifically racial stress? This percentage will likely change for each person who was involved in the event.

Dallas likely felt _____ percent relationship stress and _____ percent racial stress.

Adam likely felt _____ percent relationship stress and _____ percent racial stress.

Kevin likely felt _____ percent relationship stress and _____ percent racial stress.

Dallas's father likely felt _____ percent relationship stress and _____ percent racial stress.

Dallas's little brother likely felt _____ percent relationship stress and _____ percent racial stress.

Step 3: *Reflect* **on how the event could impact relationships.** Consider each person involved, how they were affected, and if there was anything that could have been done to ask for support or attempt to repair the relationship (in the moment or after).

Write the names of people affected by what happened.	In what ways could each person be affected?	What could have been done to ask for support or attempt to repair the relationship?
Name: Dallas		
Name: Adam		
Name: Kevin		
Name: Dallas's father		
Name: Dallas's little brother		

Now you can use the three-step relationship reflection process (describe, assess, reflect) with one of your own experiences that was racially stressful. The experience can be something that you experienced personally or witnessed vicariously. To use the three-step relationship reflection process in the future, you can download a copy of this worksheet at http://www.newharbinger.com/50676 and fill it out as many times as is helpful.

Three-Step Relationship Reflection Process

Step 1: *Describe* **the situation.** Reflect on the details of the experience (who, when, where, why) and the details that alerted you to see that the situation was related to racism or racial stress.

Who: _____

When: _____

Where: _____

Why: _____

Step 2: *Assess* **the racial stress level.** Reflect on how stressful you think the situation was and the details that were signs of stress.

On a scale of 1 to 10, with 1 being no stress and 10 being extreme stress, rate how stressful the event was: _____

What details (thoughts, feelings, behaviors) were signs of stress? _____

_____

What percentage do you think was general relationship stress and how much do you think was specifically racial stress? This percentage will likely change for each person who was involved in the event. You can start with yourself.

I felt _____ percent relationship stress and _____ percent racial stress.

Name: _____ likely felt _____ percent relationship stress and _____ percent racial stress.

Name: _____ likely felt _____ percent relationship stress and _____ percent racial stress.

Name: _____ likely felt _____ percent relationship stress and _____ percent racial stress.

Name: _____ likely felt _____ percent relationship stress and _____ percent racial stress.

Step 3: *Reflect* **on how the event could impact relationships.** Consider each person involved, how they were affected, and if there was anything that could have been done to ask for support or attempt to repair the relationship (in the moment or after).

Write the names of people affected by what happened.	In what ways could each person be affected?	What could have been done to ask for support or attempt to repair the relationship?
Name:		
Name:		
Name:		
Name:		
Name:		

more to do

Please reflect on how the experiences of racial stress and trauma have influenced your relationships.

Parents: _____

_____

Siblings: _____

_____

Friends: _____

_____

Teachers: _____

_____

Coaches: _____

_____

Other: _____

_____

After experiencing racial stress and trauma, you may trust only the people who are in your close social and family circles, and have less trust for people outside of your inner circle.

Circle of Trust Exercise. Based on your brainstorming, write the names of people who are currently inside and outside your circle of trust for sharing racially stressful experiences. If you have a hard time thinking about who would go into that circle, reflect on what someone outside the circle would need to do to be brought in.

Name the people you have healthy relationships with that you could talk to when you experience racial stress.

Name of a friend: _____

Name of a safe adult: _____

Name of a community resource: _____

PART 3

Building Your Skills for Navigating Racism

Racial stress can cause you to experience a range of emotions that may lead to you experiencing different thoughts and feelings about yourself, what it means to be Black, your relationships with others, and even about the world. It is important for you to learn healthy ways to deal with those difficult thoughts and feelings, and to identify how your individual strengths, your family, your community, and your cultural experiences are a source of strength for you that can help you overcome challenging situations. You have so many strengths and skills to help you manage your emotions. We are excited for you to spend some time in this section identifying what has helped you in the past, and for you to learn more skills to add to your tool kit.

13 ways you can be resilient

for you to know

As a Black teen, you will likely experience racial stress and discrimination. Those experiences can make it hard for you to achieve your goals, focus on your school work, and be a happy and healthy person. You and your friends may have experienced different racial situations that may have changed the way you think and feel about the world or made it hard for you to reach your goals. While racism and discrimination can be difficult and challenging, you can resist racism and be resilient.

Resilient means excelling, surviving, or overcoming despite your experience with difficult or challenging situations. Many teens who experience racism and discrimination are resilient because of the many strengths and resources that they have from their culture, family, and community. Having faith in a higher power or a connection with God and having loving and supportive family and friends can also help us excel despite our experiences with racial stress. Something else that helps when you experience racism and discrimination is feeling proud of being Black and recognizing your history and lineage that connects you to queens and kings.

Remember, just because you experience racism and discrimination does not mean that you will suffer. You will also learn ways to resist racism. Remember that you have so many gifts, strengths, and people in your community to help you with those difficult situations. You can resist racism.

Natasha, a fifteen-year-old Black girl, experienced a lot of challenges growing up. After her mother died when she was twelve years old, she was placed in a foster home. At thirteen Natasha was sexually abused by her foster mother's boyfriend and ran away. She was homeless for several years. Natasha really wanted to graduate from high school and go to college, but one day, while meeting with her guidance counselor, her counselor said, "It's okay, most of our Black students don't go to college, so you should be happy if you graduate from high school." Instead of giving up and just being happy with graduating from high school, Natasha thought about how much of an impact Black people had on the world and how much Black people could achieve, like her favorite authors, Maya Angelou, Zora Neale Hurston, and Toni Morrison. She was so proud of being Black.

Natasha was frustrated about this conversation with her guidance counselor and shared her experience with her favorite teacher, Ms. Jones. Ms. Jones agreed to help Natasha graduate and helped her enroll in tutoring classes so she could improve her grades. With Natasha's sense of pride in being Black and her teacher's support, she graduated from high school on time and went on to attend Howard University.

for you to do

Now let's identify negative situations that you may have experienced due to your race. Below is a chart of racially stressful situations that you may have experienced. Circle each situation you've experienced.

Intimidated or harassed because of your race	Told you will be unsuccessful or unable to achieve something because of your race	Not allowed to be part of a group because of your race	Experienced discrimination or someone calling you a disrespectful name because of your race
Riding in the car with an adult or friend who was treated poorly by the police because of their race	Told your name is "ghetto" or hard to pronounce	Teased about your hair texture or skin tone	Heard about or witnessed someone close to you being treated poorly because of their race

Great job reviewing the chart above and identifying situations that you may have experienced! We know that this list did not include all the situations involving racial stress and discrimination that you or someone you know may have experienced. Please use the space below to list additional negative situations that you experienced as a result of your race.

_____

_____

_____

_____

_____

more to do

You just identified some difficult and challenging situations that you experienced. Now we want you to identify what has helped you after experiencing discrimination, because what has helped you in the past can also help you when you experience discrimination in the future. In the example with Natasha, she received support from her teacher, was determined to graduate, and was proud of being Black and of the achievements and success of other Black people. Talking to someone and setting goals is important and is a great strategy to help us become successful when we experience racial stress.

Now think about the things that have helped you after you experienced racial stress. Put a checkmark next to those things that were helpful:

☐ I think about my ancestors and all that they have achieved.

☐ I get support from my parents, adults, or teachers.

☐ I have adults that care about me and help me.

☐ I think about how proud I am to be Black.

☐ I have personal goals that I am focused on.

☐ I believe I can achieve anything I set my mind to.

☐ I have positive role models and friends.

☐ I speak up or engage in activism.

☐ I have people I can talk to about my experiences with racism.

☐ I am involved in sports, groups, or other after-school activities.

☐ I have a positive self-esteem.

Remember, those things that have helped you in the past can help you in the future!

even more to do

You are doing great! We saw how Natasha was resilient in the previous example. Now let's identify how you have been resilient. Remember, resilient means excelling, surviving, or overcoming despite your experience with difficult or challenging situations. In the table below, in the left column, list the challenging situation you experienced, and in the right column, write out how you were resilient. The first chart is an example to help you complete your resilient chart.

Difficult and challenging situations	How was I resilient?
Teased because of my skin tone (called "Darkie")	I was sad and depressed at first because I thought I was ugly, but my mom told me how beautiful I am and taught me about where my family migrated from. I learned to appreciate my skin tone and my culture and now I believe "my Black is beautiful" and I am proud and love how I look.
Bullied by the other kids in elementary school because I was the only Black kid	I was sad and angry, but I went to therapy when I was twelve and now know myself better, have learned to resist racism, and am overall a happier person.

Your turn! You can do it! Write out your difficult and challenging experiences with race or racial stress and share how you have been resilient.

Difficult and challenging situations	How was I resilient?

You are learning so much! In this section, you learned what resilience is, identified difficult and challenging experiences you encountered due to your race, and identified what cultural, community, and family factors have helped you be resilient. Now we want you to learn additional strategies to help you manage those difficult emotions and unhelpful thoughts that you may have after experiencing racism and discrimination. In the next section, you will get more practice identifying your negative thoughts and learn strategies to challenge those thoughts. Let's go!

14 challenge your thinking

for you to know

In part 2 of this workbook, we discussed how your thoughts impact how you feel and behave. You practiced a lot and learned how your thoughts affect you, and now it's time for you to take it a step further and learn how to deal with those difficult thoughts. We want you to learn how to replace and challenge your unhelpful thoughts.

Fighting back and not letting those unhelpful thoughts live in your head is an important skill to learn. For example, an unhelpful thought that you may have after experiencing discrimination by a teacher at school is *I'm stupid*. That is an unhelpful thought because it is a thought that likely causes a range of difficult feelings like sadness, anger, and anxiety. We can help you learn how to replace and challenge your unhelpful thoughts, but first you have to identify your thoughts like you did in part 2.

To identify your thoughts, ask yourself, *What was I thinking when my feelings changed?* For example, when your mood changes from happy to sad or from joyful to anxious or angry, you should always ask yourself, *What was I thinking?* or *What happened right before?* Then you can label your thought pattern and keep a diary or thought log to monitor your thoughts. After you are aware of your thoughts, you can replace and challenge them. If this sounds a little confusing, don't worry. You will get lots of practice in this section. Let's get started!

for you to do

The first step in challenging your unhelpful thoughts is to identify what you are thinking. Remember, our thoughts are those statements that we say to ourselves in our head, like *I'm proud of myself* when you do well on a test, or *They are going to keep killing us* after watching the killing of an unarmed Black man in the media. Sometimes our thoughts may be true but unhelpful.

After you identify your thoughts, ask yourself, *What was I thinking when my feelings changed?* Let's practice identifying your thoughts by drawing a picture of what you were doing the last time your feelings changed after experiencing a racially stressful event.

Great job using your creativity to reflect on your feelings related to a racially stressful event.

Let's reflect more on the event.

1. What happened in the situation?

   _____

   _____

   _____

2. How did you feel before the event?

   _____

   _____

3. What were your thoughts during or after the situation occurred?

   _____

   _____

   _____

4. How did you feel after the situation occurred?

   _____

   _____

5. What did you notice about how your feelings changed?

   _____

   _____

   _____

Now draw a picture of what you were doing the last time you felt proud of being Black.

Now let's reflect more on the event.

1. What happened in the situation?

   _____

   _____

   _____

2. How did you feel before the event?

_____

_____

3. What were your thoughts during or after the situation occurred?

_____

_____

_____

4. How did you feel after the situation occurred?

_____

_____

5. What did you notice about how your feelings changed?

_____

_____

_____

Great job with identifying your thoughts and feelings and how you were impacted by these events.

The truth is, we know that it is not always easy to tell whether our thoughts are unhelpful or helpful. Just remember this: An *unhelpful thought* is more likely to cause you to become upset and distressed if you focus on it too long. A *helpful thought* may make you feel better about the situation.

Let's practice identifying helpful and unhelpful thoughts. Beside each thought in the following chart, write whether you think the thought is helpful or unhelpful.

Thought	Helpful *or* Unhelpful
I can positively change my community.	
I will never be successful as long as racism exists.	
Even though one person does not like me, there are a lot of people who support me and want me to succeed.	
Everyone hates us because we are Black.	
We will not succeed because we are Black.	
I am proud to be Black because of our history and accomplishments.	
All Black boys and men will be killed by the police. We cannot trust any of the police.	
Because of the discrimination that I witnessed in my community, I plan to become a lawyer.	

You're doing great! It's important for you to identify the difference between helpful and unhelpful thoughts because we want you to increase your helpful thoughts and decrease your unhelpful thoughts. The more you focus on helpful thoughts, the better you will feel. This may not happen immediately. It is important to acknowledge the reality of racism and how it makes you feel. While we cannot control racism, we can control how we respond.

We will talk more about responding later!

more to do

Now that you know the difference between unhelpful and helpful thoughts, let's explore and learn about common types of negative thought patterns, which we also call *thinking errors*. Let's review some definitions and examples below.

Unhelpful Thought Patterns/Thinking Errors

All-or-Nothing is thinking in extremes. In this type of thinking, there is no middle or grey area, only extremes (like you are either all good or all bad or are a complete success or a total failure).

Mind Reading is assuming that you know what others are thinking without any evidence to support it. For example, you might think, *Janay didn't talk to me, so that means she hates me.* You do not know whether Janay really hates you. You just assume that she does. It may be that Janay is just having a bad day or just found out that her mom was sick.

Catastrophizing is assuming that the worst outcome will happen. For example, because your friend was recently discriminated against while shopping, you now believe that whenever you go shopping you will end up arrested because someone thought you were shoplifting.

Minimizing is when you are unable to identify your accomplishments, success, or good things happening around or to you. Minimizing occurs when something positive happens and you do not give yourself credit. For example, you might say, "I got an A on the test because the teacher likes me." In that situation, you are unable to recognize your achievement and only believe you did well because your teacher likes you.

Those are a few of the most common unhelpful thought patterns that youth experience. Now let's see if you can match the thought on the left with the unhelpful thought pattern on the right by drawing a line to the two that match each other in the following chart.

Unhelpful Thought	Thinking Error
"She didn't talk to us, so that means she does not like us."	All-or-Nothing
"My math teacher treats Black students unfairly. All teachers are racist."	Minimizing
"I did well in the game because I was lucky."	Mind Reading
"I'm never going to graduate."	Catastrophizing

Now that you know about different types of thinking errors, take a few minutes and write out examples of some of your own thinking errors.

All-or-Nothing

_____

_____

Mind Reading

_____

_____

Catastrophizing

_____

_____

Minimizing

_____

_____

even more to do

So far you have learned the difference between helpful and unhelpful thoughts and are able to identify thinking errors. You have also spent some time identifying unhelpful and negative thoughts. Now it's time to work on identifying more positive and helpful thoughts to replace your negative and unhelpful thoughts.

The truth is, when we are down or upset and have a number of negative thoughts playing in our head, it can be hard to find positive thoughts to focus on. From this list of positive thoughts, circle the positive thoughts that you will commit to using the next time you experience a racially stressful situation and you are having trouble identifying helpful thoughts.

I am amazing!	I will succeed!	Black people have achieved so much!
Black is beautiful!	We can achieve whatever we put our mind to!	I recognize this is discrimination or injustice, and I will not let this impact my self-esteem.
Our community is supportive and I can get help to solve problems.	I can make a difference!	I am proud of myself and my community!
I matter! We matter!	I am proud to be Black because of our history and accomplishments!	I am loved and supported!

Many teens enjoy listening to music and have created their own playlists that include their favorite music artists and songs. We can also sometimes create a negative thought playlist, similar to a music playlist, with unhelpful thoughts that we repeat over and over to ourselves.

Have you ever experienced this? If so, take a minute to identify your unhelpful thoughts related to your identity or race. Once you identify your unhelpful thought playlist, identify the more positive and helpful thoughts that you can use to replace those unhelpful thoughts.

Unhelpful Thought Playlist	Helpful Thought Playlist
1.	1.
2.	2.
3.	3.
4.	4.
5.	5.

Let's practice replacing your unhelpful thoughts with more helpful thoughts in one more activity.

Another way to challenge your thinking and identify positive thoughts is by asking yourself, *If my best friend had these thoughts, what advice would I give them?* Our goal is to motivate and uplift our friends to make them feel better—that is why your advice is important.

We provided two examples to help get you started. Complete the rest of the following chart by first filling in your most recent unhelpful thoughts. Next, in the right column, pretend you are giving your best friend advice by providing them with a more helpful and positive thought to replace the unhelpful thought.

Remember, ask yourself, *If my best friend had this thought, what would I say to make them feel better and uplift and motivate them?* To practice identifying your unhelpful thoughts and the advice you would give your best friend, you can download a copy of this worksheet at http://www.newharbinger.com/50676 and fill it out as many times as is helpful.

Unhelpful thoughts	What advice would I give my best friend?
My teachers think all Black kids are stupid. I am going to fail.	You are smart. You are not a failure. You will succeed at anything you put your mind to.
I am never going to get into college with all Cs.	You did well last year and you can do well again. With the help of a tutor, you can bring your grades up.

You got so much practice in this section and have learned so much! You are doing great! You learned about helpful and unhelpful thoughts, common thinking errors that you may be experiencing, and strategies for challenging and replacing your unhelpful thoughts. In this next section, you are going to learn how to use relaxation as a strategy to manage your emotions. We are excited for you as you continue to build your tool kit.

relax before reacting 15

for you to know

It is common to experience a range of feelings when you are confronted with racism. These feelings can range from sadness, hopelessness, and disappointment to anger, confusion, and frustration. When these feelings arise, it is important to relax before reacting.

However, it is understandable that difficult experiences with racism can make it hard to relax before reacting. Although we are not always able to plan for these experiences, we are able to practice ways to remain calm when we are confronted with racial stress. Examples of strategies that may be helpful when working to better manage emotions during experiences of racial stress include:

- Deep breathing

- Engaging in distraction techniques, like counting to one hundred by sevens or reciting a calming mantra

- Taking a break from the stressful experience by taking a walk or spending time alone

- Talking to someone you can trust

Finding ways that allow you to name your feelings, sit with those feelings, and manage the feelings is important for positive emotional health. This is important because before you can identify ways of managing difficult feelings or reflecting on them, you must first develop the skill of identifying your feelings and naming them when they occur.

for you to do

Read the story below and think about how Aspen might handle this situation. Remember to keep in mind ways that Aspen can work to relax before reacting.

Aspen is a thirteen-year-old Black girl. She is the only Black girl on her tennis team, and all her other teammates are White. During a weekly practice session, Aspen and another teammate, Kasey, were matched to play against each other. Aspen has been putting in additional time practicing with her dad on the weekends, and her hard work is beginning to pay off. Aspen easily beat Kasey in their match. However, instead of engaging in positive sportsmanship after the match, Kasey slammed her tennis racket on the ground and yelled a racial slur at Aspen. Aspen instantly felt her heart racing and palms sweating, and she felt sick to her stomach. Aspen felt angry.

In the moment, she struggled to name all her feelings, but later, once she sat with her feelings, she practiced deep breathing. Additionally, Aspen recited, No one has the power to define me, *to herself. She felt hurt, angry, and disappointed in Kasey, as she thought they were close friends. Aspen talked with her dad about what she would do if something like this ever happened again.*

Please write what feelings you would have if you experienced what Aspen experienced:

1. _____

2. _____

3. _____

Rate how strongly you would feel each feeling on a scale from 1 (not strongly at all) to 10 (strongly) if you experienced what Aspen experienced:

1   2   3   4   5   6   7   8   9   10

1. _____

2. _____

3. _____

Write the order for the steps that Aspen took when working to relax before reacting. What happened first? Second? And so on.

_____ Utilized a relaxation strategy

_____ Named/identified feelings

_____ Sat with feelings

_____ Made a plan for the future

more for you to do

Learning a range of ways to respond to racism and racial stress is important for your overall health and well-being. Strategies that help you relax before reacting are useful skills for managing racial stress. Also, sometimes you will use a coping strategy and it will still be difficult to relax. Therefore, learning multiple types of strategies will increase the odds that you will be able to use a helpful strategy when needed. Below is a list of both helpful and less helpful strategies that Aspen could use after experiencing racial stress. Please circle all of the helpful coping strategies and please put an "X" over the less helpful strategies.

Positive self-talk

Name-calling or insulting

Becoming violent

Deep breathing

Taking a break

Shutting down

Going for a walk

Doing something creative to express her thoughts and feelings

Counting to ten

Pretending like she doesn't care

Talking to someone safe that she trusts

build your cultural and spiritual strengths 16

for you to know

One thing that can be helpful when you experience racial stress and trauma is recognizing and using your cultural and spiritual strengths. Sometimes people call these *cultural assets*, which are useful or valuable things or qualities that help you feel good about your culture and race. A few common ones are history, traditions, stories, art, music, and community support. You can check out more in this chapter.

All of these things help make up a community's identity, character, and customs. You can use cultural assets any time but they are especially helpful in bouncing back from or challenging identity-based stressors, such as racism. They can be an outlet to process what happened, express how you feel, make a plan for how to respond, or feel a sense of comfort. Cultural assets also help build a stronger sense of racial identity, which can prevent you from internalizing racism. These assets are different for each person but are a source of resilience, strength, and agency in helping Black youth and families resist and thrive through many events and circumstances, especially racial stressors.

What would you identify as a cultural asset? This can be anything that you value or look to, to help build resilience and strength.

_____

_____

_____

for you to do

Now that you know about cultural assets, let's look at some common ones!

Check out this list and circle the assets that you use the most now. Do you normally use them when you experience racial stressors? Then highlight or underline the ones that you want to use more when you experience racism.

Spirituality (prayer, religion, church)	Artistic expression (painting, writing)	Music (drumming, listening to music)	Communal or collective activities (healing circles, talking with a friend)
Learning about your cultural legacy and history	Asking people close to you to share their own experience (or the experiences of your ancestors) in overcoming racial stress and trauma	Emotional debriefing (journaling)	Maintaining or promoting peace and harmony among others or within yourself
Learning about and/or exercising activism and resistance	Family and kinship support and relationships	Reflecting on your beliefs and goals (values and personal goals for the future)	Racial identity (having a sense of connection and positive view of your racial group)
Having a sense of hope and vision about how you can help change things to fight for racial justice and equity	Maintaining cultural authenticity	*What else?*	*What else?*

Now let's reflect.

You may have noticed that there are two empty boxes. Those were left empty just for you! Do you have any other ideas that you would like to add to the box? See if you can think of other assets to add.

Were the ones that you circled first (the ones that you use the most now) different from or the same as the ones you highlighted or underlined (the ones that you want to use more when you experience racism)?

_____

_____

_____

Which ones do you think would be the most helpful to you after an experience with racism?

_____

_____

What could help you put these into practice?

_____

_____

_____

_____

even more to do

Now let's look at an example to consider when and how teens might use these cultural and spiritual strengths.

Mario was raised in a close-knit town in Puerto Rico where the cultural pride was clear and unapologetic. On any given day in his barrio (neighborhood), you could hear salsa music playing, the smell of delicious traditional foods like mofongo or plantains, and see Puerto Rican flags on every block. Shortly after his thirteenth birthday, his family had to relocate to Washington, DC. Although Mario was American and Afro-Latino, he felt very different from the other Black kids at his school. He often stayed quiet and tried to blend in with the other students. One day a classmate, Adrian, heard him speaking Spanish to a teacher and said, "Wait, are you Black? If so, how do you know Spanish so well?" In that moment, Mario felt anxiety about being "caught." With hesitation, Mario replied, "Well, I am Black, but I am also Puerto Rican. I identify as an Afro-Latino." After a short pause, Adrian said, "That's awesome, man, I never knew there were Black Latinos!" Mario was shocked that Adrian had never met a Black Latino before and began telling him all about his experience as a Black Puerto Rican. When Mario got home, his mom was playing music by the famous Celia Cruz, and he decided to share what happened at school. His mom reminded him of the importance of being authentic to who he is and of the richness and assets of celebrating and sharing his cultural heritage with others. Mario initially felt ashamed that he was hiding parts of his culture and language so that he could blend in with the other kids at school, but he also felt excited to know that Adrian was interested in learning more about his culture. Mario's mom suggested that he invite Adrian over to his house for dinner and dancing over the weekend.

Which assets could Mario use to process how he was feeling, and how could they be helpful?

_____

_____

_____

_____

Which assets could Mario use in the moment the next time that he feels hesitation to share or show parts of his ethnic-racial identity and culture?

_____

_____

Which assets could Mario use to promote his sense of pride? How could they be helpful?

_____

_____

_____

_____

_____

17 family empowerment

for you to know

Families are often the first place that we learn about race and culture. Within Black families, there are several common messages that come up in the process of learning about race and how to deal with racism. As you read about each one, think about if you have experienced any of these.

The first messages align with some of the things that we have been talking about already—learning about the history of your racial group; engaging in activities, talking about and seeing things that are representative of your identity (i.e., cultural pride). These cultural experiences and conversations can help build your self-esteem, identity, and well-being, and even help you when you experience racial discrimination.

Next are messages that teach youth about racism and how to respond to it. Preparation for racial bias can help you recognize racism and have strategies for how to respond. In the face of a racial stressor, these messages can also help you recognize that there is nothing wrong with you and instead there is something wrong with the larger system and individuals that show racist behaviors and thoughts.

Some adults may minimize or ignore the existence of racism and racial differences. You may hear people say they are "color-blind" or do not "see race." However, when you or others dismiss racism, it can lead to negative consequences, such as feeling confused, thinking that something is wrong with you, or experiencing a sense of hopelessness that there is nothing you can do.

Finally, as a way to protect loved ones, some families warn youth not to trust people outside of their racial group. For example, some people may directly or indirectly communicate to not trust White people. This is rooted in historical or current-day injustice and racism.

Messages preparing you for racism, building cultural pride, and teaching you to have cultural appreciation for other groups are most helpful. It is good for you to understand these common messages and recognize that people often provide these messages to prepare and protect youth.

for you to do

Have adults or peers in your life shared any of those types of messages about race? If so, write them in the box next to the message type below.

Common Messages	Example from Your Own Life Who, What, When, Where, Why?
Cultural pride—learning about the history of your racial group; engaging in activities, talking about and seeing things that are representative of your identity	My sister took me to the African American history museum when I was in ninth grade to teach me about my culture and history!
Preparation for racial bias—teaching about racism and how to respond to it	
Color-blind/evasive—minimizing or ignoring the existence of racism and racial differences	
Mistrust—warnings to be cautious around or not to trust people outside of your own racial group	

Are there other race-related messages that you can think of? If so, write them in the blank boxes.

Some teens may have little to no experience with some of these messages. However, as a teenager, you can learn new things, ask questions, research history, and ask others about their experiences! Are there certain messages that you want to learn about? Do you want to understand why your family talks with you about some topics but not others? Write out one or two questions that you have in the box below and what you could do to find out that information soon.

Questions You Have	How You Can Find the Answer

more for you to do

There are messages all around, both said and unsaid, about race. We get these from many places (school, neighborhood, social media, friends, society) and in many forms (verbal, nonverbal, representative items, cultural holidays or celebrations).

Look at the example below and notice all of the different ways that Monique received messages about cultural pride from just her family!

Monique is a fourteen-year-old girl who has a strong sense of connection and pride in her Black identity. Growing up she had many children's books and toys that had characters that looked just like her. Some of her favorite foods were the same things that her parents grew up eating. For example, she loved her grandmother's collard greens and sweet potato pie—Southern classics. She also loved when her father made saltfish and ackee, which was a common dish from his home country of Jamaica. Her mother and father had a lot of beautiful Black art around the house. Most evenings music from famous Black American and Jamaican artists flooded their home. Sunday family dinners were Monique's favorite tradition. After the family prepared their meal together, they sat around the dinner table and shared stories about themselves or their ancestors. These stories helped Monique understand her history, learn about her family's challenges and strengths, appreciate her culture and, most of all, feel proud to be Black.

What are different things that you are interested in doing to learn about your cultural history and take pride in being Black? Write them down:

1. _____

2. _____

3. _____

4. _____

5. _____

18 community engagement and activism

for you to know

A part of resisting racial stress and trauma includes your ability to recognize racism, feel that you can do something about it, and then find a way to take action against it. Let's break these pieces down a bit more.

The first step is recognition, and hopefully this workbook has given you tools to do that. Recognition also includes your ability to reflect on, analyze, and name racial injustice. You may also notice other intersecting systems of oppression or injustice (i.e., sexism, classism, heteronormativity, ableism) too.

The second step is to increase your confidence and belief that you can create change related to the racial injustice that you see or experience. This confidence will increase as you continue through the workbook and practice over time.

The third step is to engage in action to challenge or confront racial injustice, and this can be individual or collective.

The fourth step is identifying barriers to your action and finding ways to problem solve these barriers. Now let's practice applying these steps!

for you to do

Write down a racist experience, policy, or rule that is racially unjust within your school or larger community that you want to change.

_____

_____

Next, brainstorm how you could apply the four steps to move you toward activism to address this concern.

1. What could you do to critically reflect upon, analyze, and recognize the injustice or inequality?

   For example: Read books that help me better understand injustice, racism, or unfair practices based on someone's identity.

   _____

   _____

   _____

2. What would it take to build your confidence or belief in your ability to create change?

   For example: Seeing other people around me who fight for justice and make a difference in ways that are authentic to who they are.

   _____

   _____

   _____

3. What are some options for you to take action in response to the injustice? Would this be individual or collective?

For example: I could participate in a leadership group or committee working on issues related to race, ethnicity, discrimination, and/or segregation (e.g., youth organizing group) that I care about and am interested in.

_____

_____

_____

4. What are barriers that could stop you from taking action in the way that you described above?

Now identify ways to problem solve these barriers.

For example: I may not have time to go to every weekly meeting, but I could make a commitment to go at least twice a month and support the group even when I cannot be there in person.

_____

_____

_____

To practice these four steps to activism in the future, you can download a copy of this worksheet at http://www.newharbinger.com/50676 and fill it out as many times as is helpful.

more for you to do

Below is a list of action items (Aldana, Bañales, and Richards-Schuster 2019) that you could do for anti-racist engagement in your third action step. Check what you have done in the past to respond to racism or racial injustice, or check what you want to commit to doing in the future.

Examples of Engaging in Anti-Racist Action

Action	What You Have Done in the Past	What You Want to Commit to Doing in the Future
Confront a friend who uses racially charged language or makes inappropriate racial remarks, even as a joke.		
Confront a family member who uses racially charged language or makes inappropriate racial remarks, even as a joke.		
Confront an adult (such as a teacher, coach, or family friend) who uses racially charged language or makes inappropriate racial remarks, even as a joke.		
Stand up for a friend who is the target of inappropriate racial remarks.		
Stand up for a stranger who is the target of inappropriate racial remarks.		
Stop myself before using inappropriate racial remarks, even as a joke.		
Discuss issues of race, ethnicity, inequality, inequity, and marginalization with friends.		
Seek out events or meetings dedicated to discussing race, ethnicity, inequality, inequity, and marginalization.		

Action	What You Have Done in the Past	What You Want to Commit to Doing in the Future
Join a club or group focused on race, ethnicity, inequality, inequity, and marginalization.		
Pursue leadership roles (such as student council, president of a club).		
Participate in a group (such as a club or youth organizing group) to address topics of race, ethnicity, inequality, inequity, and marginalization.		
Contact media outlets (such as the newspaper, TV, or internet) when you witness offensive behavior or actions.		
Contact your elected representatives (such as city council, mayor, legislator).		
Join protests on issues related to race, ethnicity, inequality, inequity, and marginalization.		
Coordinate your own project or initiative to address issues surrounding race, ethnicity, inequality, inequity, and marginalization.		
Invite others to participate in advocacy (such as demonstrations, protests, or meetings) related to race, ethnicity, inequality, inequity, and marginalization.		
Encourage others to address issues related to race, ethnicity, inequality, inequity, and marginalization.		
Investigate social issues in my community.		

celebrate black pride and joy 19

for you to know

After experiencing racism or other racial stressors, being Black may sometimes feel like a heavy burden. You may really feel this if you are the only Black person in a class or other environment, or after you have experienced some sort of mistreatment due to your race. It is especially important during those times to remember that being Black is so much more than the stress we experience due to our race. This section will focus on celebrating Black pride and joy.

Celebrating Black pride and joy is important, as it provides balance to the difficult moments and connects you to people within the Black community, plus it's a way to remember the joy in who you are. There is pride and joy in being Black.

Black pride and joy is also the way we wear our hair, our style and fashion, or the swag we add to playing any sport. Being Black is rhythm, dancing, singing, and using our experiences to excel in school. It's also the celebrations, laughing, holidays, community, and enjoying being who we are fully. We cannot think of the experience of being Black without remembering to celebrate our Black pride and joy!

for you to do

Black pride and joy is the things that you do to help you feel supported, inspired, motivated, happy, and the events that uplift the Black community in a positive way. It is the numerous ways that we create space to celebrate the fullness of our Blackness.

There are so many ways that you can celebrate being you. When you think of celebrating Black pride and joy, what does that mean to you? Use this chart, and in each triangular piece of the whole, write out a component that defines Black pride and joy for you. Remember to bookmark this page so that you can come back to it whenever you need a reminder of the beauty of your Blackness.

Black Pride and Joy Is...

Now that you have begun to define what Black pride and joy means to you, here are some additional activities and things that you can do to reaffirm the pride and joy in your Blackness. We wanted to provide you with examples of things that you can do alone or with others to celebrate Black pride and joy. These examples are a starting place, but we have left additional blank spaces at the bottom of the chart for you to include additional ideas.

Individual How you show yourself Black pride and joy Example: Loving myself		
Reading books by Black authors	Personal style (clothing, hair)	Post or read positive and inspiring posts on social media
Shopping at Black owned businesses	Learning about my history	Having *fun* with my friends

Affirmations How you speak to yourself to instill Black pride and joy in yourself Example: I am proud of myself		
I am proud to be Black.	I am needed in the world.	I am filled with love and joy.
I believe in me.	I matter no matter what anyone else says.	I am in charge of my future.

Cultural Events *Joy in being in community with others* Example: *Cooking a family meal together*		
Attending church or religious ceremonies	Juneteenth, Kwanzaa, MLK Day, Black History Month activities	Attending an HBCU
Family reunion, cookout/BBQ	Joining a cultural organization	Learning about my family history and traditions

Creativity *Expressions of Black pride and joy* Example: *Writing (poetry, stories)*		
Creating music, raps, songs, poetry, etc.	Drumming circles	Learning African dance
Roller-skating	Dancing (alone or in community with others)	Painting, coloring, creating artwork

more to do

Let's think about when you can engage in celebrations that remind you of the pride and joy of being you! We know that you are more likely to complete a task when you have it scheduled or planned out in advance.

It's time for you to make a plan. Find a quiet place to take a few minutes and think about your upcoming week. Remember to think about what you may already have planned (school activities, family events, extracurricular activities) for the upcoming week. Now think about your schedule and if there are days that you have more time to celebrate *you*. Those are the days that we want you to schedule at least one to two activities that represent Black pride and joy into your plan for the week.

To help you, we have created an example of a weekly planner that you can use. This planner includes a column for the different types of activities and the days of the week. We have also provided an example to get you started.

After scheduling your activities, see what it's like to add celebrations into your weekly schedule. Do you notice any changes? Does it help you to feel more pride in who you are? Our hope is that over time, continuing to engage in these celebrations, whether small or large, will increase your sense of pride and encourage you to embrace your full culture, heritage and history, and racial identity.

Week 1 Example Schedule

	Activities: *Individual, Affirmations, Cultural Events, Creativity*
Sunday	Church (Cultural Event)
Monday	I matter no matter what anyone else says. (Affirmation)
Tuesday	Practice
Wednesday	Game
Thursday	Practice
Friday	Try out a new hairstyle (Individual)
Saturday	Roller-skating with friends (Creativity)

Week 1 Schedule

To help you create a schedule that includes your weekly Black pride and joy activities, you can download a copy of this worksheet at http://www.newharbinger.com/50676 and create a new schedule week to week.

	Activities: *Individual, Affirmations, Cultural Events, Creativity*
Sunday	
Monday	
Tuesday	
Wednesday	
Thursday	
Friday	
Saturday	

Week 2 Schedule

	Activities: *Individual, Affirmations, Cultural Events, Creativity*
Sunday	
Monday	
Tuesday	
Wednesday	
Thursday	
Friday	
Saturday	

PART 4

Game Plans for Dealing with Racism in the World

Although we have little control over our experiences with racism in the world, we can try to prepare for it, build resistance, and create a game plan for how to respond and heal. Racism will occur across contexts, and some of the most common contexts for teens are within your family, school, community, and with peers (teammates, friends). Hopefully, by now you have learned how to take care of yourself and others to promote healing in the face of racial stress and trauma, so this last section will help you think through and create plans for how to respond across the four places where teens spend their time. Remember, there are no right or wrong answers, and the more you practice and prepare, just like learning to play an instrument, the better prepared you will be in the moment.

20 navigating racism at school

for you to know

Unfortunately, a lot of students experience racism at school. There are times when other students do things that are racist, and sometimes adults do things that are racist. Sometimes it can be easy to tell that someone was being racist, and at other times, it may be more difficult. You might hear or see something that you think isn't right or fair, but it can be hard to tell if someone purposely did or said something to you because of your race. The important thing to remember is that if someone says something to you that you don't like, you have the right to stand up for yourself. It is also important to know that you don't have to deal with racism alone. You can always find someone you trust to help you out.

for you to do

Read the example below and think about how you might handle this situation.

Your teacher says, "Black students are so violent. That's why they are always getting suspended." You might be pretty upset if you hear your teacher say something like that. You might feel so upset that you can't even think, so you might need to tune in to what you are noticing and feeling in the moment and take a deep breath before choosing to respond. There might be other times when you feel like you cannot say something right away. It may be helpful to talk about your experience with someone first before responding.

There's not always an easy way to handle situations like this. When you get upset about something at school, it is important to think about how you can respond in a way that doesn't get you in trouble.

Who would be the first person you would talk to about this situation? (Circle one.)

Friend   Family Member   Adult   Therapist   School Staff

If the person you would talk to first is not described above, write their name here:

_____

Why did you select this person? What qualities do they have that make them a good person to discuss this situation with?

_____

_____

_____

_____

It can be helpful to think ahead about who you would feel most comfortable talking to if you experience something racist at school. That way you can feel more prepared and have a plan of action. You may not immediately know how to respond in the moment, but knowing who your support person will be is a good first step. You could also have more than one support person!

Would you tell any adults at school what your teacher said? Why or why not?

_____

_____

_____

_____

Sometimes it can be hard to know who you can trust at school. Some students may find it easy to think of a few adults at their school that they like and trust, and other students may not be able to think of any. If you can't think of an adult at your school that you would want to talk to about a teacher making a racist comment, that's okay. You just want to be sure that you can think of one adult that you can talk to, who will give you good advice about how to respond.

Now that you have had some time to think about the people who could best support you in a situation like this, choose one. Then go ask them what they would suggest you do if any of your teachers made a racist comment at school. Write down their advice below.

_____

_____

_____

_____

_____

more to do

There are times when you may think it is best to talk to someone before responding to a racist event, but there may also be other times when you want to respond immediately. For example, when you hear a racist comment or see something unfair happening to someone because of their race, you might say something in the moment. It can be helpful to have a plan for what you might say or do, so you can feel more prepared and empowered. In the boxes below are a few examples of ways that you might respond if you hear someone make a racist comment at school. Have you ever tried any of these? As you read the examples, circle any that you have tried.

A. Say something funny to break the ice and change the subject	B. Stand up for yourself and let the person know that you won't tolerate that type of treatment	C. Tell another adult at school	D. Organize a community event outside of school to increase awareness
E. Join or start a school group for students who would like to work together to advocate for change and support each other	F. Organize a school town hall meeting	G. Take some deep breaths	H. Talk to a close friend about what happened
I. Ask the person to repeat what they said and document it	J. Talk to a family member or mentor	K. Point out the flaws in what the person said and tell them it was racist	L.

There are a lot of different ways you could respond to racist events at school. Different situations may require you to respond in different ways. You may have noticed that there is one empty box. That box was left empty just for you! Do you have any other ideas that you would like to add to the box? See if you can think of another productive way to respond to a racist event at school.

even more to do

Great! Now that we have you thinking about different ways that you might respond to a racist event at school, look at the examples below and write the letter of the option from the previous table that best describes what you might do. Don't worry if the way that you would like to respond isn't listed in the previous table. It's great to continue thinking of helpful ways to respond when racism occurs.

Examples	Write the letter that best corresponds to the way you would respond.
Someone says to you, "I'm surprised! You talk so proper."	
One White student and one Black student both walk into class five minutes late without a pass. The teacher only sends the Black student to detention.	
You walk into the bathroom and see a racist comment written on the wall.	
Your school counselor discourages you from applying to the college of your choice because she thinks that it will be too challenging for you.	
A teacher tells you to stop wearing your Black Lives Matter t-shirt to school because it is too disruptive.	

There can certainly be a lot to think about if you experience racism at school! Deciding who you can talk to and how you will respond is not easy, but having a game plan is a helpful way to feel more prepared when these difficult events happen. Talking through your game plan with someone wise who you trust can be helpful too, so they can help you think through your response and maybe even practice your game plan. Dealing with racism at school is not easy, but it is easier with a game plan!

for you to know

Family relationships can include the connection you have with your parents, siblings, cousins, aunts, uncles, godparents, and godsiblings. We also know that some families encounter racist experiences collectively. Making a game plan for how to respond to racism with your family can help you feel prepared for racially stressful events.

However, having a game plan for racism with your family may be difficult. The challenges you may face will depend on who makes up your family and how much you trust them and feel safe with them. There are so many family experiences and family makeups that there is no way we would be able to cover them all in this book. For example, your game plan with your family may be different if you are a part of a multiracial family living in a diverse neighborhood compared to if you are a Black family living in a predominantly White neighborhood. The experiences may look different and may require a different game plan.

Sometimes a teen who has experienced racial stress or trauma may feel confused about who is okay to trust and who is safe. For example, say you are scrolling on a cousin's social media page and you see that they made a post that was negative about your racial group. It may feel scary to talk to that cousin about feelings or experiences related to race or racism (e.g., hearing a racial slur), even if you trusted your cousin in the past. It is common to feel vulnerable or confused about who are your safe people in your family. Generally, this makes it more difficult to maintain trust in some established relationships, or even to develop trust in new relationships.

After an identity-based stress or trauma, you may also notice changes in your mood that can impact your relationships and connections. For example, you may feel angrier or more aggressive than usual. This is sometimes because you may feel threatened or hurt by the experience. Family can feel like an easy target sometimes, and it may be tempting to release your anger by being mean or short-tempered with them. But it is important to remember that if you do this, your relationship with them can be weakened or even harmed.

Adults will want to help you with making a game plan. It is important to remember that just because a family member is older than you, that doesn't mean they are always right about what game plan is best for you. Be sure to check in with your individual needs as you identify who your safe family members are. When talking about racism, this makes for a strong game plan!

for you to do

Family Assessment Matching Activity. Please match each situation with the best family game plan for dealing with racism by drawing a line from the situation (on the left) to the grouped responses (on the right). After matching, pick one scenario to discuss with one member of your family.

Situation
Julius, a biracial boy, goes to lunch with his White grandmother and her White friend. When the waiter arrives to take their order, Julius takes some time to figure out what he wants. During the wait, his grandmother's friend says, "Don't all of you love fried chicken? Just get that."
Savannah, a fifteen-year-old Black girl, and her cousin Bre are the same age and go to the same school, a primarily White high school. At lunch Savannah and Bre hear a White student use a racial slur when singing a popular song.

Grouped Responses
The child in this situation can tell a teacher or other trusted adult about the situation. In the moment, the child in the situation can say, "I do not appreciate when you use racial slurs. They do not help me feel safe." The child in this situation can pick things that make them feel good and proud to be Black, like watching a documentary about the history of Black people or reading a book about Black history.
The adult in this situation can make a statement like, "Wow, did you just say that stereotype?" or "In the future, please refrain from using those types of stereotypes with my family. It is not okay." The child in this situation can say, "I do not like to be stereotyped. I think it is rude."

Grouped Responses

While finishing up his homework, James overhears the nightly news. James's mother is in the living room watching the most recent update on the killing of Black people due to racial hate. James hears his mom sniffling and sees that she is crying as she watches.

Situation

The adult in this situation can say, "I know it can feel scary to see mom cry. I am feeling sad about the recent news and sometimes crying makes me feel better. We can practice a coping strategy together if that's okay."

The child in this situation can say, "Mom, I see you are having big feelings about the recent news. What can we do together to feel better about this sad news?"

more to do

Here are some self-assessment questions to consider. Please rate and respond below.

Step 1. Self-Assessment and Check-In

1. How safe do you feel with your family when dealing with racism?

    Rate on a scale from 1 (not safe at all) to 5 (I feel very safe):

    1   2   3   4   5

2. What do you need from your family to feel safe when dealing with racism? If you do not feel safe when dealing with racism with someone in your family, identify one family member or caring adult you do feel safe with and discuss these feelings with them.

    _____

    _____

Step 2. Family Assessment and Check-In

1. How can you assess who is safe to talk to about racism?

    _____

    _____

    _____

22 taking action in the community

for you to know

You may notice that there are some laws, practices, or policies in your local community that negatively impact Black people. You may remember that in part 1 we talked about different types of racism. Racism in the community can be overt or covert, just like it is with individuals. Remember: Covert racism is embedded into a system, like schools or hospitals, and people aren't always aware that it is occurring. Overt racism involves intentional behavior that is harmful, like a person hitting you because you are Black.

Some examples of racism that occurs in the community are:

- Lack of resources in the Black community (e.g., fewer grocery stores to buy fresh fruits and vegetables or a lack of community centers where kids can play and learn after school)

- Higher rates of Black people getting arrested

- Black people being followed around in stores while shopping

- Someone placing a sign in their yard that says, "Go Back to Africa"

for you to do

Racism occurs all around us every day. Sometimes it is easy to see and other times it is more difficult. Take a minute to think about your community. What other examples of racism in the community have you observed? If you can't think of specific examples from your community, try to think about some examples that you have learned about. If you get stuck on this one, ask an adult you trust to help you out.

_____

_____

_____

_____

_____

_____

_____

more to do

When racism happens in our communities, we don't have to simply accept it. Taking action to change things can actually make you feel better. Some of the ways that people make changes in their neighborhood or community are listed below. Take a look at the ideas below and see what else you can add to the list.

Become mayor	Volunteer	Join a community group that is doing positive things	Participate in a rally for justice
Go to college	Encourage my friends to make good choices	Become a police officer	Mentor someone
Join the Student Government Association	Graduate from high school	Vote when I turn eighteen	Learn more about my culture and history

Now it's your turn. Can you come up with a few more ways that people can make positive changes in their neighborhood, community, or even right in their own homes?

1. _____

2. _____

3. _____

4. _____

5. _____

Now take a look at your list and the list of examples we provided for you. Is there anything on either list that you would like to do someday? Circle the examples that interest you the most.

Now list two small steps that you could take to help you get a little bit closer to one of those goals:

1. _____

2. _____

When you get frustrated by all of the negative things that are happening to Black people in your community and start to feel overwhelmed, it might be helpful to come back to your list and identify one small step you can take to make a difference in your community. No step you take is too small! Every step forward is one step closer to making a change!

for you to know

Shaniyah has been a member of the same ballet dance company since she was three years old. Although she is the only Black dancer in her group, she's never felt out of place with the other dancers, and many of them feel more like her sisters than her friends. This is probably because most of them have been dancing together since they were little girls. One day Shaniyah was running behind and entered the dance studio late. All the other dancers were talking and laughing, sounding like they were having so much fun, so Shaniyah picked up her pace to try and join in on the fun. When Shaniyah got close to the group, she realized that her "extended family" was making fun of Black ballet dancers.

"Look at the way her body looks in the leotard. I know she's probably a good dancer, but I don't think Black people should be ballet dancers," said Sarah.

"Yeah," said Elisabeth. "I agree. The muscles and dark color of the skin just throw off the gracefulness of how ballet should look."

Shaniyah was devastated. She turned around and never entered the studio. They didn't even know that she heard them. Shaniyah spent the rest of the day questioning if there was space for her in the dance world. She wanted to know if the other dancers in the dance group had similar feelings about her. Did they even understand how hurtful their comments were or that the comments were racist? Shaniyah had so many feelings and questions, but she had no idea how to move forward.

As a culture, we often don't talk about what happens when you experience racism from someone you know, especially if that person is your friend, peer, or even a teammate. However, we know that many teens experience racism that is directed toward them from their peers. These experiences may sometimes leave you with more questions than answers. You might find yourself wondering:

- "Should I address my team members as a group?"

- "Should I pull the person aside individually to address the problem?"

- "Should I talk to a trusted adult or teacher in the school or place where the incident took place?"

- "What will happen to our friendship?"

- "Should I just let it go?"

In this section, we will help you figure out the answers to some of these questions by creating a game plan for how to address racism from friends, peers, or teammates. First, take some time to think about your own experiences.

Have you experienced racism from a friend, peer, or teammate? If so, briefly describe the incident below:

_____

_____

_____

How did you handle the incident?

_____

_____

_____

Are there things you learned from that incident that you can use if it occurs again?

_____

_____

_____

for you to do

Experiencing a racist comment, behavior, or mistreatment from someone you trust, such as a friend, peer, or teammate, can trigger a lot of different and confusing feelings for you. Especially if you experienced those behaviors from a friend or if you are a student at a predominately White school. You may not feel comfortable or safe talking with anyone about what occurred. In these situations, many teens may feel that speaking up about the situation will result in being further isolated or even pushed outside of the friend group.

There are lots of different ways you can respond, and it can be overwhelming trying to decide what to do. Don't worry! We're going to work through this together. Let's start by thinking about a few steps you can take to help you figure out how to address racism from friends, peers, and teammates.

Step 1. Clearly identify what happened.

It may not always feel easy to communicate why something a friend, peer, or teammate did or said felt racist. In step 1, clearly write out the racist event and include as many details as you can remember. This may include things like:

- Where the act took place

- The person's tone of voice

- Who else was around

- Whether you tried to address it in the moment but felt dismissed

- The intention of the person (Do you think they are trying to say something to hurt you? Is it possible that they did not know that the behavior was offensive, but you still felt a lot of emotions due to their behavior?)

What was the racist act that you experienced from a friend, peer, or teammate? To help you with this step, include as many details as you can remember, including:

What happened?

_____

_____

_____

_____

What was your response? (This can include experiencing shock.)

_____

_____

_____

Where were you?

_____

Was anyone else around? If so, what was their response?

_____

_____

_____

Step 2. Identify your feelings and thoughts.

It can be difficult to identify exactly what you're feeling or thinking after experiencing racism from a friend, peer, or teammate. In many instances, there may be several different emotions and thoughts that you experience at once, or over the span of a few days or weeks. Your feelings are important and can help you identify what you may need, so we wanted to help get you started in identifying your feelings and thoughts.

Here are a few feelings someone may experience after a racist event. Identify and circle any of the feelings you experienced. Feel free to add any additional feelings to the list.

confused	hurt	angry	disappointed
fearful	numb	neutral	mad
alone	isolated	singled out	unsafe
betrayed	misunderstood		

Here are a few thoughts someone may experience after a racist event. Identify and circle any of the thoughts you experienced. Feel free to add any additional thoughts to the list.

- *I am alone.*

- *This person is not a good friend.*

- *I have people who truly love me.*

- *I can't believe my friend hurt me.*

- *I am proud of who I am despite how others may respond or treat me.*

- *Did that really just happen to me?*

- *I need to talk to someone about this. (Who can I talk to?)*

- *This person's behaviors are not acceptable.*

- *This problem is a reflection of the person's insecurities, not me.*

- *I am [add an affirmation].*

- *I hate being different from others.*

- *Things will never get better.*

- *I want to spend more time around people who love me for me.*

Step 3: Let's talk it out.

Talking to a trusted friend, adult, or even an ally can help you feel connected to others and is a reminder that you are not alone. Who are the people in your circle that you can trust to help you in times of need? Write their names in the circles below.

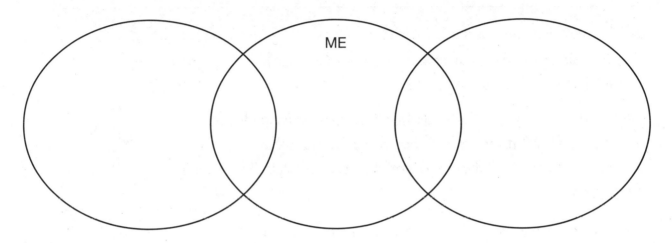

Step 4. What do I do now?

Now that you have identified the problem, you understand your feelings, and you have connected with others, what do you do?

Use the following chart to write out all the possible solutions to your problem. Write out all your options. Once you have several ideas down, consider the potential solutions. One way to figure this out is to evaluate whether the solution will address the concern. Ask yourself:

- *Is the solution helpful in getting to the outcome or resolution that you wanted?*

- *Does the solution help others to better understand your feelings or perspective with the problem or situation?*

If the answers are yes, it may be a helpful solution to try! But if the solution leads to further misunderstanding, or it doesn't really allow you to express your feelings, it may be unhelpful. Is there an additional action you can add to an unhelpful solution to help you get the outcome that you desire for the current problem or situation?

By filling out the following chart, you will have a chance to select what seems like the best choice. A copy of this chart is available at http://www.newharbinger.com/50676. When you are trying to decide whether a solution is helpful or unhelpful, download this form and complete it as often as you need.

Solution	Helpful	Not Helpful
Solution: Talk to my friend after school and tell her that her comment was hurtful to me. Why this could be helpful: This could lead to a conversation between me and my friend, it may inform her of her hurtful behaviors, and she may apologize, which may provide space to repair the relationship.	X	
Solution: Yell at my friend, tell her that she is a racist, and never talk to her again. Why this may not be helpful: My friend may not fully understand why I am yelling, she may yell back, and it leaves less opportunity for change or for talking about my feelings.		X
1. Solution: Why is it helpful or not helpful?		
2. Solution: Why is it helpful or not helpful?		

3. Solution: Why is it helpful or not helpful?		
4. Solution: Why is it helpful or not helpful?		

Step 5: Implement the game plan.

There may not be an automatic, correct solution to addressing racism, even if it occurs from one of your friends, peers, or teammates. Out of the possible solutions you identified, which one feels like the best solution to start with? Use that solution and try it out!

Step 6: Did it work?

What was the outcome of the solution? Did the solution you picked result in the change you wanted to see? If not, you have already completed the hard work of identifying alternative solutions. Select another option that you feel may also be helpful and try it again.

It is important to note that sometimes you may decide to do nothing. You may not want to address your friend and you may not want to deal with any potential consequences. That is okay. However, it is especially important that you still complete the problem-solving steps, and identify ways that you can surround yourself with community and those who love you, who help you to feel happy, and who can help you be your most authentic self!

more to do

Let's practice these skills. Come up with some solutions for handling the following situations and then decide if your solutions would be helpful or not helpful.

Situation: *A friend "jokingly" mispronounces your name and calls it "ghetto" in front of the class.*

Possible Solutions	Helpful	Not Helpful
1.		
2.		

Situation: *You are playing basketball and your teammate calls you a derogatory name (e.g., "Monkey Boy") in the midst of trash talking during the game.*

Possible Solutions	Helpful	Not Helpful
1.		
2.		

Situation: *You were on TikTok and noticed an offensive post about Black people on your friend Courtney's page. You called her and told her the post was racist and offensive and she said, "Why are you so mad? I wasn't talking about you; you're different."*

Possible Solutions	Helpful	Not Helpful
1.		
2.		

even more to do

Sometimes a friend, peer, or teammate may do or say something to you or while they are around you that is extremely racist, but the person is unaware. Maybe it was a bad joke, or it could be due to your friend not knowing the history or meaning behind a word or action. Either way the impact of the action feels the same.

We want to emphasize that not knowing that something is racist and/or hurts another person is never an excuse. But these situations do occur and may happen with someone you're really close to. This is a space for you to figure out a game plan for what you can do.

You already have a problem-solving strategy to carefully think through possible solutions to address your concerns. Here are a few potential responses you can use to start a discussion with a friend. You can feel free to take something from the list or try out a few options of your own!

Conversation Starters

It may be hard to call your friend out for doing or saying something that is racist. Here are a few ways for you to start the conversation if you decide you would like to talk about what happened:

"I want to talk to you about what you said/did."

"What you said was hurtful to me because _____."

"Did you know that using that word is actually racist?"

"The joke you said is offensive and it hurts me as your friend."

"When you said/did _____, what did you mean by that?"

What conversation starters have you found helpful in approaching a friend, peer, or teammate? Use the space below to write in additional conversation starters. A copy of this worksheet is also available at http://www.newharbinger.com/50676.

1. _____

2. _____

3. _____

4. _____

5. _____

6. _____

Actions You Can Take

Now that you have started the conversation (or not), what else can you do? Check out the list below for additional options:

- Educate your friend on why the behavior is offensive or racist

- Talk to other friends or people you trust for advice on how to talk to your friend, peer, or teammate

- Encourage your friend to educate themself around race and racism

- Invite your friend to a cultural event or program

- Decide to do nothing and choose to spend your energy taking care of yourself

- If your friend is not willing to discuss the problem or change the behavior, decide if you want to continue the friendship

What additional actions would you take the next time you experience racism from a friend, peer, or teammate? Use the following blank spaces to add more actions to the chart. A copy of this chart is available at http://www.newharbinger.com/50676 to fill out as many times as you need as you discover new actions that help you to address experiences of racism that you may encounter from a friend, peer, or teammate.

_____

_____

_____

_____

_____

_____

_____

Experiencing racism from a friend, peer, or teammate is hurtful and can sometimes make you feel that you are all alone or that you don't have any options for dealing with it. We hope that now that you have worked through this activity, you feel confident in using these tools to have difficult conversations with your friends, peers, or teammates. You also have activities that help you remember all the things that make you great!

on you go: take pride in you

Dear courageous, intelligent, and beautiful Black youth:

We are so proud of you! We know you are out here navigating the tough realities of racial stress and trauma *and* we know that is not easy work. Yet, you are doing it. We hope you are proud of yourself too! You have shown your commitment to doing this work by using your experiences, intelligence, and creativity to engage in the activities and recommended strategies throughout this book. We hope this workbook helped you get to know yourself and understand your race-related experiences better, and provided you with valuable tools to manage racial stress and trauma. Although life may continue to throw stressors your way, recognize that you have the ability to learn new skills and navigate different types of stress, including race-related stressors. The tools and skills that you've learned from this book will always be available to you. You can even share your experiences and knowledge to support others.

Now we want you to *keep going*. As you keep practicing *Skills to Help You Manage Emotions, Resist Racism, and Feel Empowered*, we hope it will help you in every area of your life. Keep showing up for yourself, keep learning who you are, keep resisting racism and other forms of oppression, keep taking the time that you need to rest and restore, and keep being authentic with yourself and others about your experiences and what they mean for you. Most of all, keep exploring the strength of your history and loving who you are—we all truly "stand on the shoulders of giants," and you are a giant in the making.

With So Much Love and Respect,

Drs. Jessica Henry, Farzana Saleem, Dana Cunningham, Nicole Cammack, and Danielle Busby

references

Aldana, A., J. Bañales, and K. Richards-Schuster. 2019. "Youth Anti-Racist Engagement: Conceptualization, Development, and Validation of an Anti-Racism Action Scale." *Journal of Adolescent Research Review* 4: 369–81.

Bryant-Davis, T. 2007. "Healing Requires Recognition: The Case for Race-Based Traumatic Stress." *The Counseling Psychologist* 35(1): 135–43.

Carter, R. T. 2007. "Racism and Psychological and Emotional Injury: Recognizing and Assessing Race-Based Traumatic Stress." *The Counseling Psychologist* 35(1): 13–105.

Clark, R., N. B. Anderson, V. R. Clark, and D. R. Williams. 1999. "Racism as a Stressor for African Americans: A Biopsychosocial Model." *American Psychologist* 54(10): 805–16.

Cohen, J. A., and A. P. Mannarino. 2008. "Trauma-Focused Cognitive Behavioural Therapy for Children and Parents." *Child and Adolescent Mental Health* 13(4): 158–62.

Elias, S. 2015. "Racism, Overt." In *The Wiley Blackwell Encyclopedia of Race, Ethnicity, and Nationalism*, edited by A.D. Smith, X. Hou, J. Stone, R. Dennis and P. Rizova. Chichester, UK: Wiley.

French, B. H., J. A. Lewis, D. V. Mosley, H. Y. Adames, N. Y. Chavez-Dueñas, G. A. Chen, et al. 2020. "Toward a Psychological Framework of Radical Healing in Communities of Color." *The Counseling Psychologist* 48(1): 14–46.

Metzger, I. W., R. E. Anderson, F. Are, and T. Ritchwood. 2021. "Healing Interpersonal and Racial Trauma: Integrating Racial Socialization into Trauma-Focused Cognitive Behavioral Therapy for African American Youth." *Child Maltreatment* 26(1): 17–27.

Katz, P. A., and J. A. Kofkin. 1997. "Race, Gender, and Young Children." In *Developmental Psychopathology: Perspectives on Adjustment, Risk, and Disorder*, edited by S. S. Luthar, J. A. Burack, D. Cicchetti, and J. R. Weisz. Cambridge: Cambridge University Press.

Roberts, A. L., S. E. Gilman, J. Breslau, N. Breslau, and K. C. Koenen. 2011. "Race/Ethnic Differences in Exposure to Traumatic Events, Development of Post-Traumatic Stress Disorder, and Treatment-Seeking for Post-Traumatic Stress Disorder in the United States." *Psychological Medicine* 41(1): 71–83.

Saleem, F. T., R. E. Anderson, and M. Williams. 2020. "Addressing the 'Myth' of Racial Trauma: Developmental and Ecological Considerations for Youth of Color." *Clinical Child and Family Psychology Review* 23(1): 1–14.

Seaton, E. K., K. M. Scottham, and R. M. Sellers. 2006. "The Status Model of Racial Identity Development in African American Adolescents: Evidence of Structure, Trajectories, and Well-Being." *Child Development* 77(5): 1416–26.

Stevenson, H. C., Jr. 1994. "Racial Socialization in African American Families: The Art of Balancing Intolerance and Survival." *The Family Journal* 2(3): 190–98.

Williamson, V., and I. Gelfand. 2019. "Trump and Racism: What Do the Data Say?" https://www.brookings.edu/blog/fixgov/2019/08/14/trump-and-racism-what-do-the-data-say.

Jessica S. Henry, PhD, is a licensed clinical psychologist in Washington, DC; and Georgia. She is cofounder and vice president of program development and evaluation for the Black Mental Wellness, Corp.; and founder and CEO of Community Impact: Consultation & Psychological Services—a trauma-informed organization whose mission is to provide trauma-informed services to individuals and organizations affected by traumatic events. Henry is current senior director of behavioral health for one of Washington, DC's largest federally qualified health centers; and was previous clinical director of a level-five close security male prison, and Georgia's largest youth homeless shelter. Overall, Henry is passionate about the mental health of individuals in Black and under-resourced communities, and has specialized in increasing access to treatment and providing the highest quality of evidence-based mental health treatment services to underserved youth, families, and adults exposed to traumatic events (e.g., community violence, abuse, neglect). She received her BS from Howard University, MA from Columbia University, and PhD in clinical psychology from The George Washington University. She is from the greater Washington, DC metropolitan area. For more information about Henry, please visit www. blackmentalwellness.com or www.impactthecommunity.com. She can also be found on Instagram @BlackMentalWellness or @CommunityImpact_CP.

Farzana T. Saleem, PhD, received her PhD in clinical-community psychology, and is an assistant professor in the graduate school of education at Stanford University. Her research examines the influence of racial stressors and culturally relevant practices on adolescents' psychological health and adjustment, with a focus on understanding the process and contextual nuance of how youth learn about race and respond to racism (often termed, ethnic-racial socialization) across families and schools. She is codeveloper of the group-based intervention, TRANSFORM, designed to heal racial stress and trauma among youth of color. Saleem utilizes research to develop applied tools and interventions that promote the mental health and development of Black adolescents and other youth of color, as well as those within their surrounding contexts. She is from Atlanta, GA; and currently lives in the San Francisco Bay Area. For more information about Saleem, visit www.farzanasaleem.com, or follow her on social media @drftsaleem on Instagram and @dr_ftsaleem on Twitter.

Dana L. Cunningham, PhD, is a licensed psychologist, and cofounder and vice president of community outreach and engagement at Black Mental Wellness, Corp. She is also program director at the National Center for School Mental Health in the department of psychiatry at the University of Maryland School of Medicine. Cunningham is passionate about increasing access to culturally responsive and antiracist mental health care for underserved youth, and uplifting the voices of marginalized populations. Cunningham also authored a children's book, *A Day I'll Never Forget*, to support children who have been impacted by the incarceration of a loved one. Additionally, Cunningham owns a private practice in the greater Washington, DC area; where she resides. Cunningham received a BA in psychology from Spelman College, and obtained her MA and PhD in clinical psychology from Southern Illinois University at Carbondale. To learn more about Cunningham, please visit www. blackmentalwellness.com.

Nicole L. Cammack, PhD, is a licensed clinical psychologist in Maryland and Washington, DC. She is founder, president, and CEO of Black Mental Wellness, Corp.; and she also owns Healing Generations Psychological Services and Consultation Center, LLC., a private practice in Washington, DC. Cammack received her bachelor's degree from Howard University, and her PhD in clinical psychology from The George Washington University. Throughout her career, she has continually focused on mental health issues specific to the Black community, and identifying ways to address the cultural and systemic issues that impact Black mental health and wellness. She currently lives in Washington, DC. For more about Cammack, please visit www.blackmentalwellness.com or www. healinggenerationscenter.com.

Danielle R. Busby, PhD, is a licensed clinical psychologist; and cofounder and vice president of professional relations, and liaison of Black Mental Wellness, Corp. She is assistant professor in the department of psychiatry and behavioral sciences at the University of Texas Medical Branch. Busby's research and clinical expertise are centered on youth suicide prevention and intervention, decreasing barriers to care for underserved populations, and child trauma—including racial trauma among Black youth. She is passionate about continuously bridging the gap between research and clinical practice, and committed to amplifying and supporting marginalized voices through education, clinical training, and healing. Busby was born in Detroit, MI; and raised in Southfield, MI. She received her BA in psychology from the University of Michigan, and her master's and PhD in clinical-community psychology from The George Washington University. For more about Busby, please visit www.blackmentalwellness.com or www.drdaniellebusby.com.

Foreword writer **Howard C. Stevenson, PhD**, is Constance Clayton Professor of urban education and professor of Africana studies in the Human Development and Quantitative Methods Division of the graduate school of education at the University of Pennsylvania. He is executive director of the Racial Empowerment Collaborative.

More ⏱ Instant Help Books for Teens

An Imprint of New Harbinger Publications

THE RACIAL TRAUMA HANDBOOK FOR TEENS

CBT Skills to Heal from the Personal and Intergenerational Trauma of Racism

978-1648480126 / US $17.95

Journal

PUT YOUR WORRIES HERE

A Creative Journal for Teens with Anxiety

978-1684032143 / US $18.95

THE MINDFUL BREATHING WORKBOOK FOR TEENS

Simple Practices to Help You Manage Stress and Feel Better Now

978-1684037261 / US $17.95

OVERCOMING SUICIDAL THOUGHTS FOR TEENS

CBT Activities to Reduce Pain, Increase Hope, and Build Meaningful Connections

978-1684039975 / US $18.95

FINDING HER VOICE

How Black Girls in White Spaces Can Speak Up and Live Their Truth

978-1684037407 / US $16.95

THE SELF-CONFIDENCE WORKBOOK FOR TEENS

Mindfulness Skills to Help You Overcome Social Anxiety, Be Assertive, and Believe in Yourself

978-1648480492 / US $18.95

◐ new**harbinger**publications

1-800-748-6273 / newharbinger.com

(VISA, MC, AMEX / prices subject to change without notice)

Follow Us 🔲 f 𝕏 ▶ 𝓟 in

Did you know there are **free tools** you can download for this book?

Free tools are things like **worksheets**, **guided meditation exercises**, and **more** that will help you get the most out of your book.

You can download free tools for this book— whether you bought or borrowed it, in any format, from any source—from the New Harbinger website. All you need is a NewHarbinger.com account. Just use the URL provided in this book to view the free tools that are available for it. Then, click on the "download" button for the free tool you want, and follow the prompts that appear to log in to your NewHarbinger.com account and download the material.

You can also save the free tools for this book to your **Free Tools Library** so you can access them again anytime, just by logging in to your account! Just look for this button on the book's free tools page.

+ Save this to my free tools library